This Book Is Dedicated To
All The Sun Employees
Of The First 100 Years

Centennial Celebration
The Story of Sun Company

1886 1901

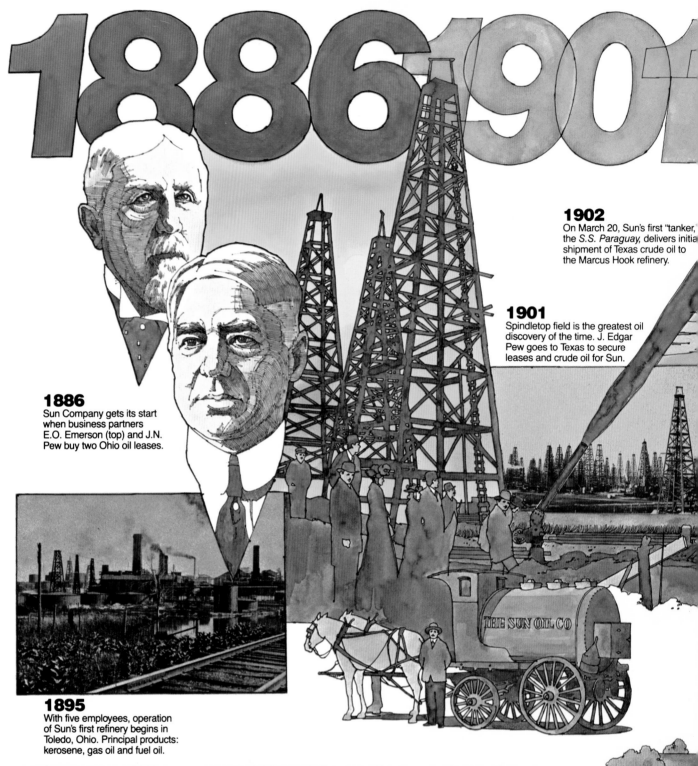

1902
On March 20, Sun's first "tanker," the *S.S. Paraguay*, delivers initial shipment of Texas crude oil to the Marcus Hook refinery.

1901
Spindletop field is the greatest oil discovery of the time. J. Edgar Pew goes to Texas to secure leases and crude oil for Sun.

1886
Sun Company gets its start when business partners E.O. Emerson (top) and J.N. Pew buy two Ohio oil leases.

1895
With five employees, operation of Sun's first refinery begins in Toledo, Ohio. Principal products: kerosene, gas oil and fuel oil.

1901
J.N. Pew purchases 82 acres at Marcus Hook, Pa., as site of second Sun refinery; operations begin in March 1902.

"Working for Sun Company these years has been not merely a job. It has been participation in an exciting adventure — a way of life providing satisfaction in the accomplishment of our goals. So our people have become a great team, welded together by great ideals and purposes accepted by each of us."

J. Howard Pew — 1956

The Joy of Originating

Edward Octavius Emerson

"*Working for Sun Company these years has been not merely a job. It has been participation in an exciting adventure — a way of life providing satisfaction in the accomplishment of our goals. So our people have become a great team, welded together by great ideals and purposes accepted by each of us.*"

J. Howard Pew — 1956

Some things are still the same. Some aren't.

People still put pies on the windowsill. Our ancestors did it to cool them. We do it to thaw them.

Parents still worry when the children leave the house. Our grandparents wouldn't allow the kids to cross the street on their skates. We encourage them to cross an ocean in a jet.

Americans still treasure their freedoms. Our forefathers explored, with curiosity, society's capacity for achievement. We test, with caution, the world's willingness to live in harmony.

The 1886-1986 time period permitted the people of this planet to sort out some of what worked, and what didn't. It was a period of productivity and turbulence, of high expectations and low international boiling points. This was the climate for the evolution of Sun Company from an idea in Lima, Ohio, to one of the world's most successful industrial enterprises.

The learning curve of 100 years tells us that Sun's strength did not come from constant uniformity, historical habit or people who all thought alike. This celebration of a century required a continuous flow of bright minds, vigorous ideas and professional points-of-view — often at odds with each other.

What emerged with each passing decade was a company that held on to the old just as long as it was good, and reached for the new just as soon as it was better.

Before a company can proudly count its years, it must prove that it has something else to count. Sun's "something else" is a remarkable litany of achievements as a producer of economic growth, technological advancement and social improvement. In the process, Sun developed some beliefs, some values, that add up to something called "the character of the company."

That character has been shaped through the lessons of these past 100 years. You'll encounter those

Sun Chairman Theodore A. Burtis (left) and President and CEO Robert McClements, Jr., (right) with portrait of company founder Joseph Newton Pew.

"lessons learned" throughout the pages of this book. Among them:

■ *The Joy of Originating* — You get a strong sense of innovation from the "firsts" Sun has brought to its industry. What's made that happen is a passion for adventure, the quest for the new, the search for something better. You can find it in a geologist studying a map in the wilderness; in a refinery operator bringing a new plant on stream; in a chemical engineer working late in a laboratory.

■ *The Influence of Example* — Most of us are one part original and three parts what we learn from those who have gone before us. A Spindletop field boss, early in this century, wrote to the men in his crew and advised them to "work hard, help each other, pay your bills and kiss your wife every day." Sun has always been rich with people who taught us about style, about ethics, about attitude.

- *The Power of Perseverance* — The Sun dreams that have come true happened because people stuck to their ambitions. They did not let occasional disappointment get the upper hand, nor did they cut and run at the first sign of adversity.

- *The Dignity of Work* — Success for Sun has never been a matter of luck. It's been a willingness to work, to compete, to understand that you must do your work better than the person in a competitor's house doing the same job.

that 100-year line it became evident that Sun would be a special kind of company, with care for its customers, its employees, its shareholders, its community, its country. For the question: "Why did you do that?" there is no better answer than "Because it was the *right* thing to do."

- *The Worth of Character* — For a century Sun people have experienced *the joy of originating, the influence of example, the power of perseverance, the dignity of work, the productivity of teamwork, the excitement of*

The Lessons of a Century

- *The Productivity of Teamwork* — Sun people have always understood that they were part of something larger than themselves — that what they did combined with what others accomplished added up to a triumph all could enjoy.

- *The Momentum of Enthusiasm* — Enthusiasm has been the pilot light of Sun's progress. It converts a scientist's confidence into a commercial reality. It anticipates a marketing trend and meets the demand. Sun has been gifted in every decade with people eager to get on with the excitement of this business.

- *The Virtue of Patience* —The nature of our business requires employees and shareholders who understand the relationship between time and success. Success comes because we earn it, because we've learned to stay with this game for the long haul.

- *The Obligation of Duty* — Sun learned early that it must fit well into the rest of society, to participate in the agenda of a community. The millions of dollars of contributions to deserving causes, and the millions of hours of volunteer work done by Sun employees provide testimony that the company understands the need to balance its commitment to providing energy with the parallel obligation of promoting a better life for the communities we live in.

- *The Value of Tradition* — Nobody knows where habit ends and tradition begins, but somewhere along

enthusiasm, the virtue of patience, the obligation of duty, the value of tradition. The sum of all this is character.

Nobody can guarantee the future, not for the next quarter nor the next generation. The best we can do is size up our chances, calculate the risks and estimate our ability to deal with them. Sun people have done that, and have made superb choices for a century.

Years from now when people dust off this book, we hope they will see it as a tribute to the Sun employees of the first 100 years . . . for that's what it's meant to be.

We hope they will see it as a recitation of the roots of an enterprise . . . for that's what it is.

We hope they will understand that it's the launch point for what's ahead . . . for that's what it should be.

Ted Burtis
Chairman

Bob McClements
President and CEO

The Joy of Originating

Edward Octavius Emerson

Joseph Newton Pew, Sr.

The early 1900s. Sun Company's refinery at Toledo, Ohio.

The cinder-loaded handcar was heavy; the trio of workmen was having a difficult time pushing it. When a volunteer offered a helpful shoulder, the men were grateful but a little surprised—grateful for the assistance, surprised by the identity of the volunteer. He was Joseph Newton Pew, Sun Company president.

At Toledo they also tell how the company founder could wield a sledge hammer. It goes back to the day when a worker was pounding spikes into railroad ties and glanced up to find Newton Pew an interested onlooker. It wasn't long before the latter had the sledge and was demonstrating his own spike-hammering technique.

"Learned it in the oil fields," Pew explained with a grin.

He didn't start out to be an oilman. But by the turn of the century, Joseph Newton Pew was on his way to becoming one of the greatest.

"The names of several of the heavenly bodies were considered; but Mr. J. N. Pew liked the word 'Sun' on account of the sun's size; hence the name 'Sun' was adopted for the new company."

Robert C. Pew—1920

Robert Cunningham Pew was just 24 years old in 1886 when his uncle Joseph Newton Pew asked him to travel to Ohio to scout the possibility of securing leases in the northwestern Ohio oil fields. Robert, the son of Newton's brother, Thomas, had been working in his uncle's Pittsburgh oil and gas business since he was 18 and had impressed his uncle with his maturity and judgment.

Robert wasn't in Ohio very long when it became apparent to him that these new discoveries offered exceptional opportunities. Based on his optimistic report, Newton Pew and his business partner, Edward O. Emerson, directed Robert to buy oil leases.

On March 27, 1886, he paid $4,500 for two oil leases in Findlay Township near Lima, Ohio, for the purpose of oil exploration, drilling and production.

Pew and Emerson's decision to buy the two

In Findlay Township, Ohio, Robert Pew bought first oil leases for Sun. Later, he became the Toledo refinery's first manager, a post he held for 30 years.

These nine men worked in Sun's production department when the company drilled its Bluffton, Ohio, oil field in 1897.

leases was strictly a business determination; they wanted to diversify their natural gas company. At the same time, though, it was indicative of the foresight and prudent risk-taking that became characteristic of the company born of that move.

For with their entry into the Ohio oil fields, Newton Pew and Edward Emerson wrote the opening lines of the Sun Company story.

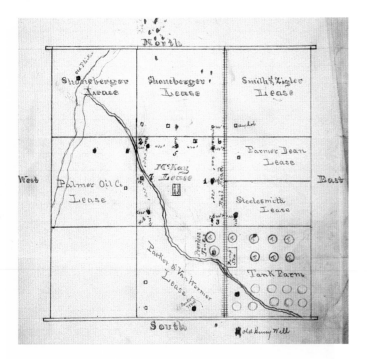

Red dots represent producing wells in this 1889 map E.O. Emerson sent to Newton Pew, outlining terms of purchase for some Ohio oil wells.

Initially, the partners continued to devote most of their attention to their natural gas business, leaving Robert to run the Ohio oil operations. Those activities, however, soon overshadowed the rest of the business, and in 1889 the two men incorporated the Sun Oil Line Company to acquire pipelines, leases, storage tanks and tank cars. This was the first time the name Sun was used in connection with a Pew/Emerson enterprise.

As the operations of the Sun Oil Line Company grew, the partners thought it prudent to consolidate the company's increasingly scattered operations. On March 17, 1890, they incorporated the Sun Oil Company (Ohio) for purposes of "producing petroleum, rock and carbon oil; transporting and storing same; refining, purifying, manufacturing, shipping, selling and marketing such oil and its various products . . ."

Joseph Newton Pew, Sr.
President 1901-1912

He was at work at his desk that October morning in 1912 when he was attacked again by his chronic heart condition. That afternoon Joseph Newton Pew died in his Sun Company office there in downtown Philadelphia. He was 64.

For 26 years he had steered this company he had helped to establish. Sun was on solid ground now. He had amicably bought out his only partner. Brought his three sons and several nephews into the business. And he was by all measures a very wealthy man.

Newton (as he was always called) started life on a hardscrabble dirt farm in the backwoods of western Pennsylvania.

He taught in a one-room schoolhouse for three years and used the money he saved teaching to further his education. Then he went into the real estate business at age 22 and opened his own office. In conjunction, he ran an insurance and loan service.

Five years later, Newton Pew was worth $40,000 and felt secure enough to get married. On Dec. 16, 1874, he wed Mary Catherine Anderson, daughter of Rebecca and Enoch Lucius Anderson.

He was always moving ahead. It probably had something to do with being the youngest of 10 children and having to struggle to keep up.

It also had something to do with the Presbyterian work ethic in which the family was raised. Newton Pew was always known to his associates as a God-fearing man with an inner drive and a highly developed set of morals.

He was 28 in 1876 when he set up partner-

Mary Anderson Pew

Newton Pew grew up in this farmhouse two miles south of Mercer, Pa. Pews were among the area's first settlers.

ship with Edward O. Emerson, a banker and Union Army veteran. The partnership, designed to pipe and sell natural gas, evolved 10 years later into the founding of Sun.

Along the way, Newton and his wife produced three boys and two girls. He was known as a de-

. . . with students at London, Pa., one-room school. Newton began teaching at age 18 and taught for three years. The money he earned enabled him to further his education.

voted family man who always had time for his home life. Most summers he took his family back to the Mercer, Pa., homestead, which he had bought, and he worked at improving the old farmhouse where he was born.

He also had time to help start a college in that area. One of his students from the old one-room school, Isaac Ketler, grew up to be an ordained minister with a dream of founding a college. He sought backing from Newton Pew and between them they established and guided an academy that grew into Grove City, Pa., College.

Though conservative in his dress, his religion and his private life, Newton

Pew had an abiding interest in the innovations of his time, both in business and in his personal life. He was one of the early owners of a touring car, but is said to have had words with his driver once when the speed topped 15 miles an hour.

In his will he left all his shares of Sun in a 20-year trust for his wife and children. By doing so, he almost ensured that they would continue to operate his company in their own best interests.

The company's assets were already considerable in 1912. Sun was producing oil in four states. It operated pipelines and tankers and two refineries. Its name and branded products stood for quality in many foreign countries.

I t was back in 1876 when Joseph Newton Pew first went into partnership with Edward Octavius Emerson to pipe natural gas to drilling sites around the oil fields of Bradford, Pa.

Pew was 28 years old and just starting to make a name for himself in the business community around western Pennsylvania. Emerson, at 42, was 14 years older, a successful Titusville, Pa., banker and veteran of the area's financial skirmishes.

Emerson brought to the enterprise money and business experience; Pew contributed youthful enthusiasm and managerial talents. They shared an affection for playing the business game.

Their natural gas business prospered and early in 1881 the partners formalized their operation by incorporating Keystone Gas Company. Emerson was president; Pew was treasurer.

Keystone Gas was so successful that a year later the two men incorporated the Penn Fuel Company to provide natural gas to the city of Pittsburgh. They were the first to supply natural gas to a major city for home and industrial use.

In 1884 the partners sold their interest in Penn Fuel and formed a new company, The Peoples Natural Gas Company. It was soon after that Pew and Emerson heard about the promising oil discoveries in Ohio, the first significant new production outside the Pennsylvania oil fields, and decided to investigate the business opportunities.

This latter half of the 1880s in the United States was a time of discovery and invention that led to the foundation of much of America's basic industrial might. The majority of Americans still lived and worked on farms but the country was beginning to gradually move away from its agricultural past. It was in the 1880s that America's love affair with the free enterprise system began to flourish.

One of the areas that was starting to provide abundant possibilities was the petroleum industry.

"When Newton Pew arrived in 1882, few Pittsburghers realized they were in need of natural gas. The Penn Fuel Company immediately embarked upon correcting this oversight by building gas pipelines to the city."

Faith and Freedom
J. H. Pew Biography

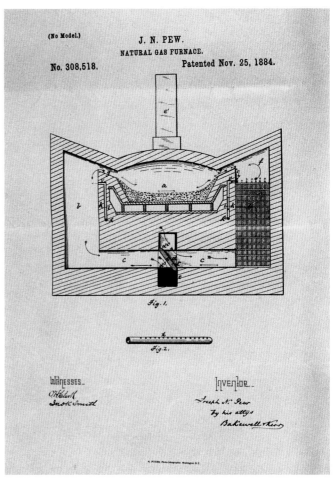

In addition to this natural gas furnace, Newton Pew also patented a gas well pump and gas meter.

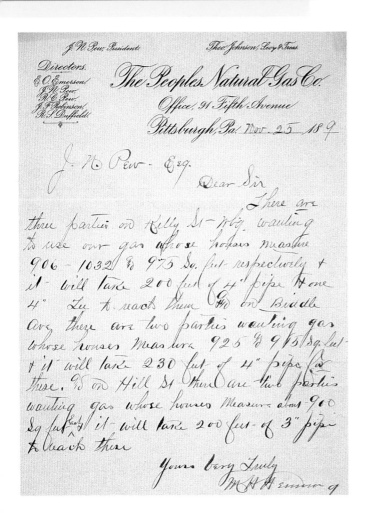

In 1859 Edwin L. Drake had drilled the world's first oil well in Titusville, Pa. Twenty-seven years later the industry was still characterized by something of a gold rush mentality, as people of every type tried to get a piece of the action.

From the beginning, two sorts of individuals were involved in the oil business—those who looked on it as a speculative, get-rich-quick venture and those who saw in it the possibility of a stable industry. The men who had enough vision to foresee future opportunities laid the foundation for the development of a new American industry.

PNG once had 4,000 customers, 100 miles of gas main and supplied 20,000 cubic feet of gas a day.

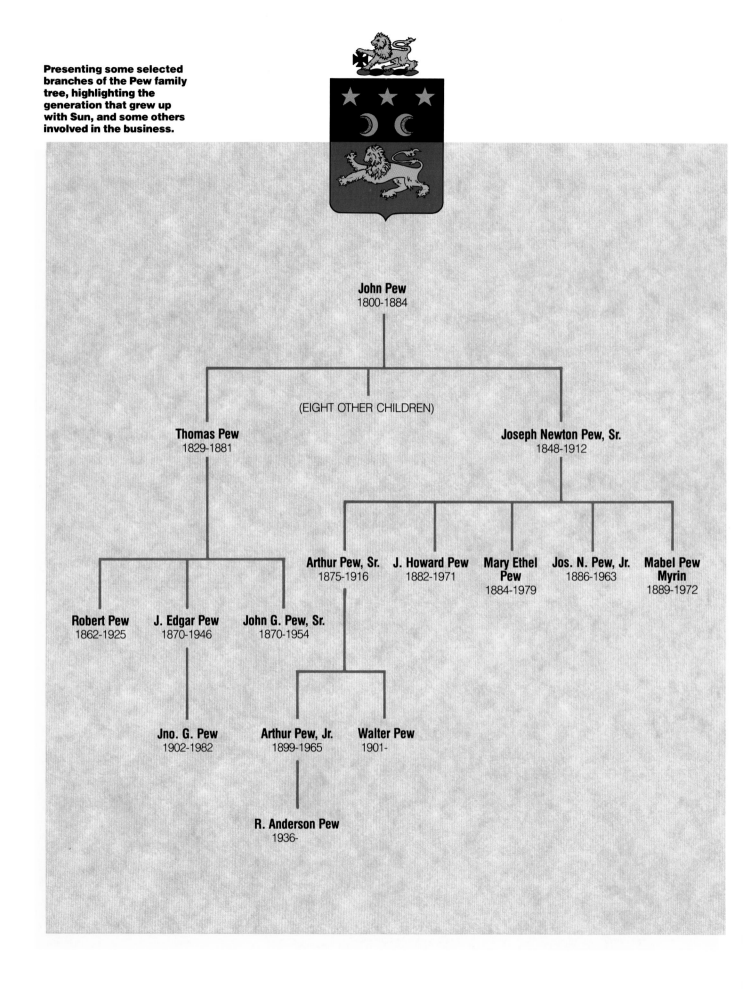

Presenting some selected branches of the Pew family tree, highlighting the generation that grew up with Sun, and some others involved in the business.

John Pew
1800-1884

(EIGHT OTHER CHILDREN)

Thomas Pew
1829-1881

Joseph Newton Pew, Sr.
1848-1912

Arthur Pew, Sr.
1875-1916

J. Howard Pew
1882-1971

Mary Ethel Pew
1884-1979

Jos. N. Pew, Jr.
1886-1963

Mabel Pew Myrin
1889-1972

Robert Pew
1862-1925

J. Edgar Pew
1870-1946

John G. Pew, Sr.
1870-1954

Jno. G. Pew
1902-1982

Arthur Pew, Jr.
1899-1965

Walter Pew
1901-

R. Anderson Pew
1936-

Joseph Newton Pew was born on July 25, 1848, just 11 years before Drake drilled his well. His hometown of Mercer, Pa., was only 40 miles from what was later to be the center of oil production in western Pennsylvania.

He was the youngest of 10 children born to John Pew, a farmer, and Nancy Glenn Pew. His grandfather, also named John Pew, and his grandmother, Elizabeth Vaughn Pew, were among the early settlers in Mercer County.

When he was 22, Newton Pew opened a real estate office in Mercer. It wasn't long before he decided that the small, quiet community didn't offer ample opportunity to a young man anxious to get ahead in the business world. So he moved his operations to Titusville, a town still caught up in the wonder of Drake's oil find.

By the mid-1870s Newton Pew had become involved in the oil and gas business, trading in property and leases. He also invested heavily in pipeline certificates, which, in effect, were warehouse receipts for oil.

In 1875, he purchased a large number of these receipts on the Titusville exchange. To do this, he used his own savings and also borrowed $20,000. Unfortunately, in this case certificates had been issued for more oil than was in storage and Pew lost his savings, plus the borrowed $20,000. Although discouraged, he remained in business and eventually paid back his creditors.

It was an unaccustomed setback for the young businessman, but from it he learned a valuable lesson that was to guide all of his future business actions: Take risks only if they are wise . . . and never do something simply because everyone else is doing it.

The experience also greatly influenced his later financial management of Sun.

"The company operated very conservatively from a financial point of view," says Donald P. Jones, retired senior vice president of finance.

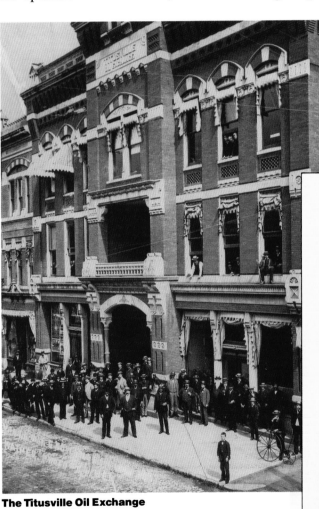

The Titusville Oil Exchange in the late 1800s.

J. N. PEW.

REAL ESTATE

BROKER.

OFFICE:

Cor. Pine and Franklin Sts.

I am always prepared to sell the best

**Business Property,
Building Lots,
Dwellings.**

OIL LANDS, OIL WELLS,

AND

Unimproved Lands,

In Crawford, Warren, Venango and Forrest counties.
may4   J. N. PEW.

Newton Pew inserted many ads like this in the *Titusville Herald* during the early 1870s.

In 1898, this Sun ad appeared in Derrick's Handbook of Petroleum.

Eight years after Robert Pew acquired the first Ohio oil leases, Sun achieved another milestone in the Buckeye State.

On Dec. 10, 1894, with Merriam and Morgan Paraffine Company of Cleveland, Sun incorporated the Diamond Oil Company to purchase for $22,200 a refinery on the outskirts of Toledo from the failing Crystal Oil Company. From that plant, Sun shipped the first oils it produced.

The property covered 14 acres, and the work force numbered five men, but soon increased to 27. The principal products were kerosene, gas oil and fuel oil. Robert Pew was refinery manager.

Eventually, Pew and Emerson bought out Merriam and Morgan and in December 1895 the property was conveyed entirely to Sun.

It is to the old Diamond Oil Company that Sun traces its current trademark, a diamond pierced by an arrow.

It was about this time that Newton Pew began considering the future direction his business should take. He had done well in the natural gas business, but he sensed that the petroleum industry offered greater challenge and opportunity.

Octagon-shaped office building was site of company headquarters in Toledo from 1902 until torn down in 1935.

Moreover, he and his partner of 23 years, Edward O. Emerson, did not always agree on how their time and resources should be allocated between the two businesses.

In 1899, Pew bought out Emerson's interest in the Sun Oil Company (Ohio), and in 1903 Pew sold his interest in The Peoples Natural Gas Company.

Henceforth, Joseph Newton Pew was to be an oilman—exclusively.

The origin of the Sunoco diamond can be traced to 1894, when J.N. Pew and E.O. Emerson formed the Diamond Oil Company to purchase a refinery in Toledo.
The diamond soon appeared as a trademark with the words "Sun Oils." An arrow was added as a device to attract motorists when Sun began marketing a full line of Sunoco motor products in 1920.

Group of Toledo office employees, circa 1909.

Sun's first branch warehouse in Detroit in 1900.

J. Edgar Pew got off the train carrying a gun, a circumstance that said more about the place than about the man. His relatives had insisted he have the gun for protection, because this wasn't just an ordinary boomtown. This was Beaumont, Texas, in 1901, shortly after an Austrian engineer named Lucas punched a hole in the southeast Texas earth and struck oil. Anthony Lucas' Spindletop well gushed 100,000 barrels of oil a day for 10 days. In 1901, it was the biggest oil find ever.

J. (for James) Edgar wasn't the first member of the Pew family to venture into the heady atmosphere of turn-of-the-century Beaumont. His brother Robert had already been to Texas to investigate lease possibilities, repeating the role he had played for his uncle Newton Pew in the Ohio oil fields.

Robert was enthusiastic about the opportunities but much less so about Texas itself. After a month in the state he returned to Toledo. Newton Pew then sent J. Edgar to Texas, a fortuitous coming together of man, place and circumstance. For J. Edgar Pew was to become one of the best known

J. Edgar Pew (left) tersely captioned this 1901 Texas photo: "Pew, Hostetter and Hostetter's bottle."

During the Beaumont oil rush, finding oil was often easier than finding lodgings. A solution: "sleeping tents," which cost 50 cents a night.

and most respected oilmen in the production end of the business.

When he died in 1946, one tribute to J. Edgar said that "his many and varied contributions to the production and conservation of oil were of untold value to the petroleum industry and the nation."

That agreeable association had its beginning that day in 1901 when Pew got off the train in Beaumont and came face-to-face with a particularly virulent case of oil fever.

Edwin M. Cage, a retired Sun legal vice president, calls J. Edgar Pew's Spindletop assignment "the start of the Production Division in Beaumont. Mr. J. Edgar was sent down to see about getting acreage for storage and contracts to buy oil," Cage says. "He was shrewd enough to see that you could make more money by drilling and producing the oil than by going around and buying it."

One of J. Edgar's first actions was to buy 42 acres of land near Smith's Bluff on the Neches River. Here, at what he called Sun Station, he erected storage tanks, which were serviced by a new pipeline from the Spindletop fields.

On May 30, 1902, J. Edgar attended a public auction called to sell off the assets of the bankrupt Lone Star and Crescent Oil Company. His offer of $100,000 was the day's only bid and it got him the prize. However, terms of the sale required an immediate down payment of $25,000.

In later years, J. Edgar liked to tell how he got the money. He said he started by going to two local banks he had been dealing with but found them closed because of the Decoration Day holiday.

As he walked the dusty Beaumont streets, pondering the seriousness of the situation and feeling his earlier good fortune slipping away, he passed a group of men remodeling an old building that was to house another bank. He described his dilemma to the man inside who immediately wrote J. Edgar a cashier's check for $25,000. J. Edgar's and Sun's reputations for reliability and fair dealing were already well-known in the industry.

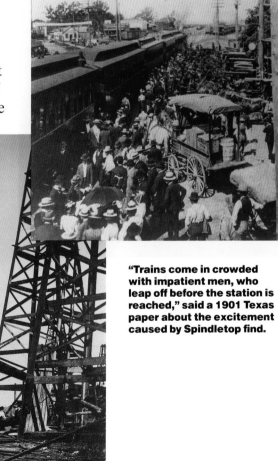

"Trains come in crowded with impatient men, who leap off before the station is reached," said a 1901 Texas paper about the excitement caused by Spindletop find.

Lindenthorpe Park once occupied the site of Sun's Marcus Hook refinery.

A 1905 management meeting on the porch of Lindenthorpe mansion. Frank Cross (left) joined Sun in 1898 as a bookkeeper, was secretary-treasurer until 1946. Oliver C. Pudan was the first manager of the Marcus Hook refinery.

S.S. Paraguay carried first shipment of Spindletop crude to Marcus Hook.

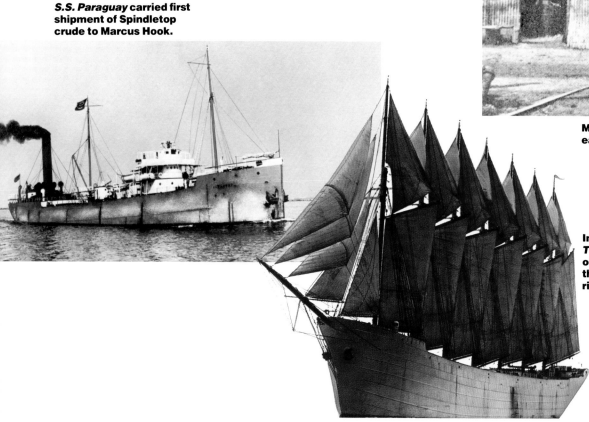

Marcus Hook refinery in the early 1900s.

In 1905, Sun converted the *Thomas W. Lawson* into an oil carrier. The *Lawson* was the world's largest schooner-rigged sailing ship.

p north, Newton Pew had taken the first steps toward upgrading his company's refining capability. The first Texas crude had been sent to Toledo in tank cars for processing.

However, Pew knew that continuing to ship Spindletop oil overland to Toledo would mean prohibitive transportation costs. On his first trip to Spindletop, Robert Pew had pointed out that one key to success there would be the ability to move the oil inexpensively to refineries.

"These are busy times at the oil plant of the Sun Company. The tract of land is rapidly presenting the appearance of a big oil refinery."

Chester (Pa.) Times
March 28, 1902

In October 1901, Newton Pew purchased land on the Delaware River and set about building a refinery to receive and process oil from Texas. United Gas Improvement Company of Philadelphia, a customer of Sun in Toledo, was a 45 percent partner in the project.

Earlier that year, on May 2, Pew had incorporated the Sun Company in New Jersey. Officers of the new company were Joseph Newton Pew, president; his eldest son, Arthur Pew, vice president; legal counsel, W. S. Miller, treasurer; and Pittsburgh associate Frank Cross, secretary.

Newton Pew bought the land at Marcus Hook from Philadelphia attorney Charles A. Chase for $45,000. At the time, it was the site of Lindenthorpe Park, a popular resort for residents of the Chester, Pa., area, featuring a beach, a half-mile race track, dancing pavilion and picnic grounds.

What made the property especially suitable as a refinery site was its location on deep water, its proximity to railroads and the refineries and pipeline terminals already at Marcus Hook.

Newton Pew wrote: "My new work at Marcus Hook has taken so much of my time that it has been impossible for me to get a day away . . . I have bought 82 acres with a thousand foot front on the Delaware River in the Borough of Marcus Hook. There is an old pier there, but I am remodeling and enlarging it. We shall be prepared to receive and deliver oil there . . ."

Construction started in November 1901, when Elwood Worrilow, a carpenter and builder hired as labor foreman, and Dave Hardy, a laborer, drove the first stakes for a railroad spur to the docks.

Four months later, the refinery was far enough along to receive the first shipment of Texas crude, which arrived March 20, 1902, aboard Sun's first "tanker," the *S.S. Paraguay*, a converted Great Lakes ore carrier.

J. Howard Pew

**President 1912-1947
Chairman 1963-1970**

He remained a bear of a man, even in his later years.

Tall, and broad shouldered, with bushy eyebrows, he was often seen clutching an enormous cigar in his fingers as he moved about Sun's corridors.

He was intense, sure of himself and deliberate in his speech even in old age.

He was probably a bit lonely in his later years because he had outlived most of his contemporaries — he was 89 when he died in 1971, still active and still coming into his downtown Philadelphia office. He took a long walk around his estate each morning and took Wednesday afternoons off for golf.

"Golf keeps me alive," he once remarked.

Investigate the personality of the young J. Howard Pew and a warm, almost engaging man emerges:
■ The young man who once said with a smile that he rushed through high school and finished at 14 because "I never liked classes." Then he finished college at 18.

Howard Pew at age 18, when he graduated from Grove City College.

■ The college graduate who slept right at the company labs so that he could more readily get back to work on his formulas and processes to develop commercial uses

. . . on the golf course in 1941. He played slowly and usually made the shot exactly the way he wanted.

for newly discovered Spindletop crude.
■ The Sun president who in 1926 instituted a matching funds program so employees could buy stock and share in Sun ownership.
■ The young man who could entertain endlessly from his memorized collection of limericks.
■ The man who even after 40 years in the company still knew hundreds

of refinery workers by name and could ask about their children, also by name.
■ The man who would sit by the hospital bed of an injured worker and stay there for hours because he felt personally involved.

This, then, was J. Howard Pew, the man who more than any other shaped Sun through an active career spanning some 70 years.

He joined his father's

company in 1901 and accepted the presidency when his father died 11 years later.

A case might have been made for naming his elder brother, Arthur, president. It was Arthur who had set up a network of sales outlets, including very profitable European branches. But Arthur was in ill health when their father died and he himself died four years later.

So J. Howard, graduate of Grove City College (with some later engineering courses at M.I.T.) became president of Sun. And his younger brother, Joseph Newton Pew, Jr., became vice president. The year was 1912. Howard was 30; Joe was 26.

Between them, they developed Sun into one of the giants of the American industrial scene. Two world wars, the Depression, numerous recessions — nothing stopped their gradual, but persistent climb.

The brothers considered themselves a team and they enjoyed each other's company, both during and outside the business day. But there was never any doubt that Howard was the designated leader.

Howard knew his role and his role was to provide primary leadership for the Sun organization and the Pew family. He did both from 1912 until he died.

. . . appearing on radio news program with Lowell Thomas. Sun sponsored Thomas' broadcasts from 1932 until 1948.

. . . attending 1945 Marcus Hook refinery employee picnic with nephew Arthur E. Pew, Jr. (center).

In 1915, Sun shipped its Red Stock lubricating oil from Marcus Hook to customers in wooden drums.

In the 16 years since the adventure started, Sun Company had grown considerably. The company that began with two Ohio oil leases now included two refineries, transportation and storage systems and an important new source of crude oil.

In 1901, Newton Pew's son, J. (for John) Howard Pew, joined the company. It was at the Toledo refinery in 1901 that the 19-year-old Howard Pew began experimenting with a process for profitably using the heavy black residue that remained when Spindletop crude was refined.

The work started at Toledo, continued at the new refinery at Marcus Hook and led to the development of Sun Red Stock, a lubricating oil that quickly won worldwide acclaim and,

One of the tank wagons used in the distribution of Sun products at Detroit in 1907.

more than any other product, laid the basis for the company's early success.

More breakthroughs followed. In 1904, thanks to the diligent work of Howard Pew and his team of researchers, Sun marketed the first commercially successful petroleum asphalt. Called Hydrolene, it was the company's first trademarked product. By 1910, Sun had more than 100 trade-name items on the market.

The company made major advances in all areas of the business—production, refining, marketing, transportation. Among other achievements ahead, Sun would market its products abroad, make significant contributions to its country's defense during two World Wars, establish a major shipbuilding facility, take on the challenge of Canada's tough Athabasca oil sands and solidify its reputation as a good neighbor and concerned citizen.

In 1908, Howard's younger brother Joseph Newton Pew, Jr., became a Sun employee. The two brothers would be associated with Sun for most of the next 70 years, leading the company along a path of success and service to become one of this nation's major corporations.

Newton Pew incorporated Sun Company in New Jersey in 1901. Headquarters were in Pittsburgh until 1904, when the company moved to Philadelphia.

In 1922, shortly after the firm entered the retail marketing arena, the name was changed to Sun Oil Company to achieve better identification with its business.

In 1976, the company assumed its original name, becoming once again — Sun Company.

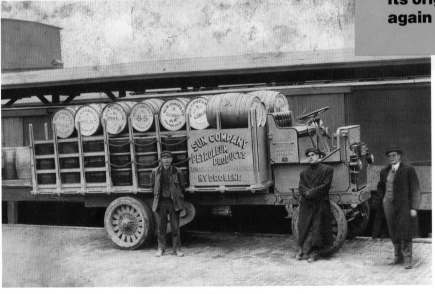

Sun's Hydrolene was a product right for its times — the first petroleum asphalt was much in demand during the early 20th century expansion of the nation's highway system.

The Power of Perseverance

born in
freedom

working for
progress

1859 OIL'S FIRST CENTURY 1959

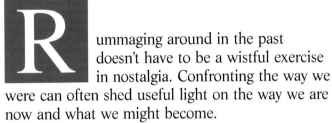

Rummaging around in the past doesn't have to be a wistful exercise in nostalgia. Confronting the way we were can often shed useful light on the way we are now and what we might become.

In 100 years, a multitude of memories can be stuffed into a scrapbook. Open the book and the recollections spill out. Sun's scrapbook is like that. In the century that the company has been part of America's energy story, we've gathered a lot of remembrances — about people and events, projects and promises.

All of them are meaningful. But occasionally there comes an event that's special. Special because it was the first, the biggest, the most innovative or because accomplishing it took an extra measure of courage and confidence.

Herewith, some historical Sun turning points.

The event that sparked the creation of Sun Shipbuilding and Dry Dock Company was a 1915 business trip J. Howard Pew took to Germany. It was an idea that would launch one of the world's greatest commercial shipyards and more than 600 ships, spark new shipbuilding technology and help the United States through two world wars.

In Germany, Howard Pew was greatly impressed by German naval and air strength. He accurately foresaw the devastation German sea power would wreak on Allied shipping, including oil tankers.

To assure a reliable, long-term source of ships to transport its crude and products, Sun began building Sun Ship in April 1916 on the banks of the Delaware River below Philadelphia at Chester, Pa. In addition to being a landmark in vertical integration, the action underscored Sun's desire for operating independence.

Sun Ship's first vessel, the *S.S. Chester Sun,* slid down the ways in October 1917. By the end of

January 27, 1917 — Workers lay the keel plate for the *S.S. Chester Sun.*

Sun Ship waterfront in 1919. After some lean times in the '20s and '30s, the yard emerged in World War II as the largest private shipyard and single biggest producer of oil tankers in the U.S.

Joseph (left) and Howard Pew (third from left) joined other dignitaries at 1917 launching of the *S.S. Chester Sun,* the first vessel built by Sun Ship.

World War I on November 11, 1918, the yard had built six tankers, plus three mine sweepers for the U.S. Navy.

Over the years Sun Ship emerged as one of America's largest privately owned shipyards, and among its most innovative. In 1923, Sun Ship introduced the Sun Doxford diesel engine, and eventually became the biggest American manufacturer of large marine diesel engines. The first all-welded tanker, the S.S. *White Flash,* was launched at Sun Ship in 1931.

World War II marked Sun Ship's glory years: an average of a ship a week rolled down its 28 ways — three on one single day. By the end of the war, Sun Ship produced more than 250 ships — 40 percent of all U.S. tankers built. The yard converted, armed and repaired 1,000 more ships and developed the T-2 tanker, backbone of America's wartime petroleum shipping supply system. During those years, Sun Ship employed 33,500 people.

Former Sun Chairman H. Robert Sharbaugh describes this period in Sun's history as one of "fierce patriotism. Making money wasn't really important — winning the war and protecting the democratic lifestyle was."

With the end of World War II came an abrupt decline in ship construction. Soon the bad years were outnumbering the good for U.S. commercial shipbuilders, as foreign competition took its toll.

"The introduction of this engine has met with almost instantaneous success," said a 1923 publication, when Sun Ship brought out the Doxford diesel engine.

In 1976 Sun Ship built a new dry dock to accommodate vessels weighing up to 400,000 deadweight tons.

October 30, 1917 — *Chester Sun* slides down the ways.

In 1943, Sun Ship received a Maritime Commission award . . . then went on to celebrate by launching three ships in less than an hour.

Sun Ship from the air, 1945.

Comedy team of Gracie Allen and George Burns paid 1944 visit to the yard to help launch *S.S. Hubbardton.*

On a river once chockablock with them, the only commercial shipbuilding yard remaining on the Delaware by 1975 was Sun Ship. By the end of 1980, Sun Company's efforts to keep its shipbuilding subsidiary alive had resulted in five-year losses totalling more than $200 million.

On a gray January morning in 1981, Sun announced that what was once one of the world's greatest shipyards was going out of the ship-building business.

The word came directly from Robert H. Campbell, then Sun Ship president, now head of Sun Refining and Marketing Company, because "the employees deserved to hear it from me."

The second announcement — on February 8, 1982 — was anticlimactic: the sale by Sun Company of all assets of Sun Ship to a Pennsylvania affiliate of Levingston Industries of Orange, Texas. A 66-year saga had come to an end.

Landman to the stars

Former E&P executive Harold Rudel recalls that as a young Sun landman in Michigan in the late '40s he used to deal with a big landowner named Russel Carter. Mr. Carter talked a lot about "his son the actor," an unknown who called himself Charlton Heston. "Later on some of the land passed to Charlton and I took a lease from him," says Rudel.

Taking on the gasoline Goliaths

Ask Al Cariello about Sun's competitive marketing spirit and the retired executive remembers battling the giant companies for a decent share of the market back before World War II.

"The volumes we put through those eyebrow stations you wouldn't believe," he says. "I mean, here's a 50 or 60 foot front with a little building and we were pumping 80,000 or 90,000 gallons a month. Used to drive the competition crazy."

Picture this

Glen Burroughs, retired president of Sun Production Company, once had the privilege of visiting J. Howard Pew in his office.

"His office was very austere," Burroughs says. "I remember there was a hole in the carpet just inside the door. There were only two pictures in his office; one of Herbert Hoover and the other of Billy Graham."

One swell (and determined) scout

Some Texas retirees still talk about Uncle Jess Hamilton, the Sun oil field scout who wouldn't stay fired. Nobody knows just what Uncle Jess did wrong, "but it must have been bad," because almost everybody got a second chance in those days. Though fired in no uncertain terms, Uncle Jess just continued scouting wells and turning in his reports. After about a month, they say, J. Edgar Pew put Uncle Jess back on the payroll.

Fathers don't always know best

Mr. & Mrs. J. Howard Pew were married in Pittsburgh in 1907. Helen Pew later said that her father, a successful businessman, had noted with approval that his new son-in-law could drive a car, which would enable Howard to earn a living driving a truck in case the oil business should fail.

Ring around the oil field

Buddy England remembers that back in the old days Sun was known in the Texas oil fields as "Edge Oil Company."

"We were never given a lot of money to buy leases with," so Sun wound up with marginal land. "I could pretty well find our leases just by driving the edge of a field," he says.

You could tell a salesman's territory by the color of his suit

Retired Sun marketing man Frank Bjornsgaard says that in some ways the company is different today than it used to be. "When I went to work for Sun in 1949, you wore a hat," he says. "This was part of the job. You wore a suit, no slacks and jacket. You wore shoes with laces. If you worked in the Western Marketing Region, you wore a blue suit."

Deep in the heart of . . . where?

For many years, the oil field operations around Beaumont, Texas, were some of the brightest stars in Sun's southwest sky. But for young Bob Anderson, born and bred in the northeast, "All I knew about Texas was where it was and the name of the capital." So when he was offered a summer job working in Beaumont, he could only ask, "Where is that?"

When Anderson retired more than 30 years later as president of Sun Gas Company, he had spent most of his Sun career working in the southwest and even had a touch of a Texas accent.

Hook, line and Custom Blending

In 1944, John Lee Olsen joined Sun as a chemical engineer. He retired 38 years later as a senior vice president. But he says "I didn't realize that I was getting involved in a career at Sun until I started to get in on the ground floor of such exciting projects as Custom Blending. Then I knew I was hooked."

Just one essential question

When Sun Chairman Ted Burtis was heading up Houdry Process Corporation, he negotiated a merger with another company. At a meeting to discuss the deal with Houdry shareholder Joseph N. Pew, Jr., Burtis recalls "The only question Joe asked was 'Is it in the interest of the employees?' He never asked about the economics. He just wanted to know if it would be good for the employees."

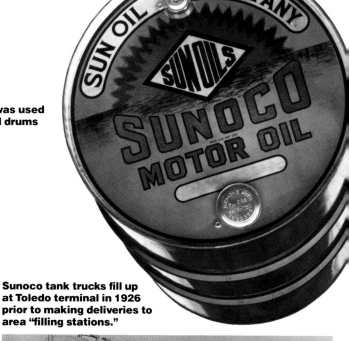

"Sunburst" design was used on Sunoco motor oil drums from 1923 to 1928.

O ne problem Sun did not in great measure share with other early 20th century refiners was what to do with one largely useless by-product of kerosene production — gasoline. The small quantities of gasoline refined by Sun at Toledo were sold locally, and there had been no incentive to increase production.

Until World War I, Sun had built its niche in the petroleum industry on its superior lubricating and

Sunoco tank trucks fill up at Toledo terminal in 1926 prior to making deliveries to area "filling stations."

Company inspectors visited Sun stations in the 1920s and '30s to check on service and station appearance.

industrial oils and on its gas oil sales to Philadelphia's United Gas Improvement Company and other customers. However, for various business reasons, during the war Sun severed its relations with U.G.I. Consequently, Sun now had large quantities of gas oil on hand, which it could use to manufacture gasoline.

Other compelling reasons fueled Sun's decision to reach out to retail automotive markets. A cottage industry in the early years of the 20th century, automobile manufacturing was now big business. By 1918 America's patchwork of highways carried more than six million vehicles.

In December 1919, the Sun board authorized spending $20,000 to construct the company's first "gasoline filling station" at Ardmore, Pa., a Philadelphia suburb. The first Sunoco-brand gasoline, stored in four above-ground tanks, was sold in 1920 from a single two-pump island.

Off to one side, a diamond-shaped sign proclaimed "Sunoco GASOLINE oils," its arrow pointing over the tiled roof of the tiny station with its arched "eyebrow" entrance, an architectural feature that would distinguish Sunoco stations and welcome customers for decades to come.

In the 1930s, "thought-fulness of the dealer" was an important part of "Sunoco Service."

At a cost of $20,000, Sun built its first "gasoline filling station" in Ardmore, Pa., a suburb of Philadelphia. It opened in 1920. More than 50 years later, a Sunoco service station still claimed the corner for Sun Company.

D id a honeymoon trip and a Chinese temple really have anything to do with the blue oil dye used by Sun in 1927 to set its gasoline apart from that of the competition?

About that time, most refiners routinely added tetraethyl lead to their gasoline to prevent engine knock.

Sun didn't have to. It produced a high-quality, no-knock gasoline from gas oil without adding lead. Unfortunately, Sun could distill only 5 to 7 percent of each barrel of oil into gasoline. Growing in the gasoline marketing business meant coming up with a more efficient refining process.

That problem was solved when the first high-pressure cracking units were installed at the Marcus Hook refinery in 1922. Now, with its gasoline being produced at much higher rates, Sun could expand its marketing territory beyond a small, mid-Atlantic region.

Most no-lead refiners sold their anti-knock premium fuels at three to five cents a gallon above their regular grades. Sun took a different tack.

In April 1927, Sun introduced its one and only

In 1931 "Mercury Made" motor oil joined Blue Sunoco at Sun's service stations.

Great for winter driving
SUNOCO
ANTY-NOK GAS | MOTOR OIL
Stops knocks-Starts quickly | The low cold test oil

This scene appeared in a Sunoco-made movie promoting the sale of gasoline coupon books. The 1925 film played in Philadelphia theaters.

In the late 1930s, Walt Disney cartoon characters appeared on billboards touting the distinctive features of Sunoco oils.

"You got something there!"
SUNOCO OIL
KEEPS MOTORS KNOCKLESS

"More gasoline must be marketed this year," said a 1930 company publication. "The man at the pump is the man who can do it."

Piece of tile from China's Temple of Heaven. Was it the inspiration for Sunoco Blue?

To show the quick starting qualities of Blue Sunoco, Sun in 1933 suspended a car beneath a plane for a mile-high flight into the clouds. In zero cold aloft, the engine started in a split second.

grade of gasoline as "Blue Sunoco — The High Powered Knockless Fuel at No Extra Price."

In the 1920s, customers could see the gasoline they were buying in the clear glass reservoirs that topped gravity-fed service station pumps. Adding color to their gasolines was one way refiners distinguished their products. At Sun, the liquid pumped distinctively blue.

Legend has it that the astral blue decided upon for "Blue Sunoco" matched the color of a tile chip from the roof of China's Temple of Heaven. Joseph Newton Pew, Jr., and his wife, Alberta, had been given the chip by their hosts while honeymooning in China in 1916.

Today, the tile chip from the Temple of Heaven resides in a special case in the lobby of Sun's corporate headquarters building in Radnor, Pa.

Joseph Newton Pew, Jr.

Vice President 1912-1947
Chairman 1947-1963

Young Joe Pew received his mechanical engineering degree from Cornell in the spring of 1908.

He had two things waiting for him:
■ an assured job at Sun, because his father owned the company.
■ a berth on the U.S. Olympic team, which was going to England that summer, because he had been captain of the Cornell track team and national intercollegiate hammer-throwing champion.

Joe later said he had been looking forward to the Olympic experience with "thoughts in mind of some pleasant weeks in the English countryside."

But Joe Pew's father had thoughts of his own concerning this youngest of his three sons. His thoughts did not include England or the Olympics.

While it was no doubt disappointing to miss the trip, young Joe didn't dwell on his father's decision. Years later, he recalled that spring of 1908 and said simply: "In a few more weeks I went to work for Sun."

Joe also remembered that after three months he went to see his father because his entry position in Sun's purchasing department seemed to be going nowhere.

"Can't you give me a real job?" he asked.

The elder Pew responded with words that his son never forgot: "Joe, you have been given your opportunity and it is up to you to make your job."

Joseph Newton Pew, Jr., buckled down and started learning the oil and gas business. It meant five nights without sleep while bringing in a new Illinois well; driving eight-ox teams with loads of pipe through West Virginia mud; laying a 20-mile stretch of solid-mahogany corduroy road in Venezuela . . . all of which helped to prepare

Joe Pew as captain of Cornell's track team in 1908. As a senior, he was also intercollegiate hammer throwing champion.

him for 55 years of Sun service, first as vice president on the death of his father in 1912, and later as chairman until his own death in 1963.

He became Sun's idea

man. The innovator. The challenger. He pushed and he prodded and along the way it was Joe Pew's direction that added notable contributions to an already innovative company heritage. Among them:
■ Sun Shipbuilding and Dry Dock Company, which he organized with his brother, Howard, to build tankers for World War I. Joe was the yard's first president.
■ The first pipeline ever constructed to transport gasoline and other refined

products, one of the industry's outstanding technological advances.

■ A combined gyroscopic instrument and high speed camera which could be lowered into an oil well to measure angle and drilling direction.

■ Establishment of Sun's unique Custom Blending system for selling different grades of gasoline through a single service station pump.

Outside of Sun, Joe Pew's consuming interest was politics. His political involvement, however, was never rooted in personal promotion. He always vigorously opposed political favors for those who gave financial support to candidates.

He once wrote to a midwestern publisher that "I have only one ambition and this is to preserve a free country for

... visiting the Marcus Hook auto lab in 1940. Joe Pew maintained an interest in the technical side of Sun's business throughout his working life.

the next generation."

As he neared the end of his career, Joe Pew spoke to a gathering of 900 Sun employees and told them that his decades with the company "have been busy years filled with happiness that comes only from work and friendships that have been cemented by time."

... testing tar seepage in South America early in his Sun career.

Arthur Pew . . . announced the breakthrough.

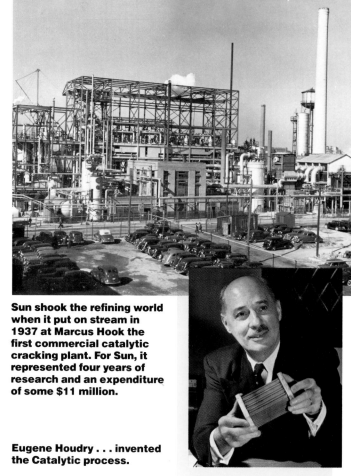

Sun shook the refining world when it put on stream in 1937 at Marcus Hook the first commercial catalytic cracking plant. For Sun, it represented four years of research and an expenditure of some $11 million.

Eugene Houdry . . . invented the Catalytic process.

There have been few revolutionary breakthroughs in petroleum. The industry is one that grew by evolution — from horses to horsepower, from wooden derricks to steel rigs, from onshore to offshore.

But the Houdry process was something different. It was a revolution in refining.

And Sun had it.

Sun's refining genius, Arthur E. Pew, Jr., announced the Houdry breakthrough to a Chicago meeting of the American Petroleum Institute in 1938 — and the refining of gasoline has never been the same.

Until that time refiners made products such as gasoline, kerosene, heating oil and fuel oil by heating crude to extreme temperatures and condensing the vapors back into various liquids. The gunky leftovers were made into a variety of low-profit items. The problem with this process was that it resulted in 60 percent gunk and only about 40 percent high-grade fuel.

Then one day in 1933 a bald, stocky Frenchman in his early 40s, named Eugene Houdry, made an appointment to see the people in charge at Sun's headquarters in Philadelphia.

Houdry offered the basics of an invention that would get more gasoline out of a barrel of crude oil. And it was gasoline of a much higher octane

quality than refiners were getting at that time. Houdry had done a lot of preliminary work back in France and at Vacuum Oil's refinery in Paulsboro, N.J. He seemed to be on to something.

In the meantime, Vacuum had gone through a merger with Socony, and Houdry's refining process got lost in the subsequent reorganization. With Socony-Vacuum's blessing, Houdry was trying to peddle his new refining process to other oil companies. So far without success.

Until he got to Sun.

Houdry later said that he talked to Arthur Pew for only 20 minutes before they struck a bargain. Pew remembered that it was more like 40 minutes.

Houdry called it the most beautiful day of his life.

Within a short time, Sun set Eugene Houdry up in its Marcus Hook, Pa., labs and he perfected a working model that functioned with precision.

"The damned little thing always did exactly what

it was told," Arthur Pew told a business reporter.

Sun then built a refining plant at the Marcus Hook refinery that covered most of a city block, gave the plant a secret shakedown for a year-and-a-half and then announced success. Many of the engineering developments which led to that success were the work of Clarence H. Thayer, then Sun's chief engineer.

It all happened just in time to meet the high-octane requirements of aviation fuel in World War II, notes retiree Jos. T. Wilson, Jr.

"The aviation gasoline produced by the Houdry process made a major contribution to the war effort," says the former director, vice president and treasurer.

During the first six months of 1945, when war needs were critical, the Marcus Hook refinery shipped more than 1.1 million barrels a month of 100-octane aviation gas.

The persistence of an expatriate Frenchman and the vision of Sun's executive management had paid off in a way that none of them could have foreseen 12 years before.

"I am pleased to report that Sun Oil Company's Marcus Hook refinery today blended for shipment to the armed forces its billionth gallon of aviation gasoline since Pearl Harbor. This achievement is the result of the unswerving devotion to duty of every man and woman of Sun's organization."

Dec. 16, 1944 telegram —
J. Howard Pew to the Petroleum Administrator for War

Proud moment: Billionth gallon of aviation gasoline produced at Marcus Hook is withdrawn by Robert Connell, a foreman at Marcus Hook. Watching are A. W. MacMurtrie (left) refinery manager, and L. B. Wells, superintendent.

"War that runs on oil" demanded—and got—best efforts of everyone at Sun.

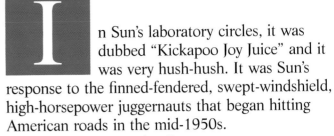

In 1956, Sun test marketed its Custom Blending system in Orlando, Florida, and invited the public to "name your own octane."

I n Sun's laboratory circles, it was dubbed "Kickapoo Joy Juice" and it was very hush-hush. It was Sun's response to the finned-fendered, swept-windshield, high-horsepower juggernauts that began hitting American roads in the mid-1950s.

"It" was Custom Blending.

By the early 1950s, Sun's single grade of gasoline could not satisfy the octane needs of the higher-compression engines being turned out by Detroit in increasing numbers.

"We were losing some market share because of this," recalls retired company Vice Chairman Robert W. Donahue of the time when he was fuel development leader for Project "Kickapoo Joy Juice."

"KJ was the code word and there were only a couple of people in the laboratory who knew what that meant," he explains.

Developing the pump fell to Einar Young at Sun's Newtown Square, Pa., research labs, and Al Marsh from marketing. Fuels development went to assistant research director Charlie Thomas.

No one had ever built a pump that could dispense multiple grades of gasoline. Einar Young found inspiration coming at odd times and places.

"I solved one of the problems while I was in church," he says. "The priest was saying Mass and

Einar Young . . . developed Custom Blending pump.

In the 1970s Sun successfully merged its gasoline marketing with growth of convenience stores.

all of a sudden the answer came to me. Another time, I was driving on the Pennsylvania Turnpike. I was thinking about the pump and I missed my turnoff by two exits.

"You don't sit down at your drawing board and suddenly this thing comes out," he says. "There was a first design, then a second, then the third. About the fourth design was the one we put in Florida."

What was tested at Sun's Orlando, Fla., stations in 1956 was dress rehearsal for gasoline marketing history. For the first time, motorists could choose the gasoline that was right for their cars from among five grades dispensed by a single pump.

Instead of pushing the sale of premium grades, the system encouraged motorists to work down to the lowest-priced product their engines could use and still be knock-free.

After the remaining kinks were worked out with designs five, six and seven, and a six-grade pump created, Custom Blending was introduced throughout Sun territory in 1958.

John Moxey, who was then assistant director of research and development of motor products, likens it to buying a hat or a pair of shoes.

"I guess you could say that what we were doing was offering gasoline in a variety of sizes."

"*Sun Oil Company, with a 'weakness' for doing the unusual, has instituted, at 17 retail service stations in Florida, an epoch-making step in supplying motor fuels to motorists.*"

*Petroleum Engineer
April 1956*

Old and new in gasoline pumps . . . from early gravity-flow model (left) to 1958 Custom Blend pump.

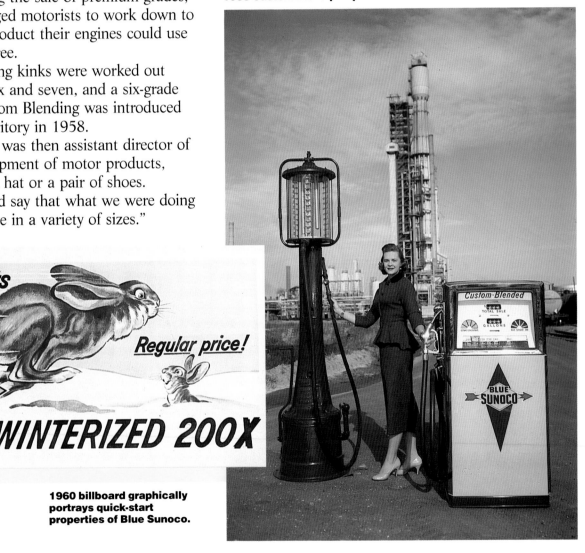

1960 billboard graphically portrays quick-start properties of Blue Sunoco.

Since it was first used in 1894, Sun's diamond has emblazoned an imaginative variety of company promotional items and gifts, from mugs to maps, from ink blotters to Indy car replicas, from gas pump telephones to tank truck models.

I f it weren't for its far northern location . . . If it weren't for the testy economics of world energy supplies . . . And if it weren't for the necessity of moving hundreds of thousands of tons of sand a day . . . Canada's Athabasca mother lode would be the best and most reliable source of energy in the world. There is more recoverable oil locked in those sands than in all of the Middle East — some 300 billion barrels in a 30,000-square-mile area.

Even the earliest settlers in western Canada knew of its location. The trick was to dig the sand, boil the oil out of it and get it to market — all in a commercially acceptable manner.

Sun was interested in the sands as far back as the 1940s. Singly and with other companies it worked on developing the technology. Then, as others dropped out, Sun found itself alone.

"I think there was great reluctance on the part of many people in Sun to see the project falter," Darwin W. Ferguson told the press in 1967. At the time, Ferguson was vice president and director of both Sun and its subsidiary, Great Canadian Oil Sands Limited.

"So after extended discussions, we made the decision to back the project," said Ferguson, who retired in 1975.

At the dedication of the plant at Fort McMurray, Alberta, Canada, in September 1967, J. Howard Pew, who was then 85 years old, told Canadian political and industrial leaders that a company

such as Sun has to have a major challenge once in a while to keep its corporate muscles toned.

"My associates have conceived and built this magnificent plant. And so I trust that they now take comfort in the knowledge that they have not become soft and that they are most useful," the old man said.

The plant was indeed a model of engineering. The company was proud of itself.

However, for almost a decade pride was replaced by the reality of economic factors in the world's energy marketplace. They warred against the success of this plant, built to boil 45,000 barrels of oil a day out of the Athabasca sands.

The "world's first oil mine," as the press referred to it, constructed at a cost of almost $300 million, became a financial drain. The plant management encountered severe operating difficulties trying to keep the facility running in some of the harshest winter weather the area had ever suffered. Temperatures hit 50 below zero and stayed there.

Before the oil sands facility finally turned the economic corner 10 years later, Sun's directors considered closing it down many times.

But, says Kenneth Heddon, who directed Sun's Canadian operations in those days, Sun considered the hardship that closing would wreak on the plant workers and the townspeople.

"So every time we took a look at it we backed off and said the alternative to closing is somewhat

worse than continuing to fight it through," he says.

Eventually, the scarcity of energy resources, combined with the upgrading and upscaling of the plant, improved the economic picture. And this first venture into unlocking oil from the Athabasca sands became a financial contributor to Sun.

Other than J. Howard himself, the most enthusiastic proponent of Sun developing the sands was Clarence Thayer, who provided the leadership in the technical areas.

At completion, Sun's complex on the Athabasca River was the world's first commercial venture to produce synthetic crude from the oil sands.

Bucketwheel excavators are used to mine the oil sands.

Its oil scrubbed out, the moist and rich-looking oil sands become the clean, white powdery granules found on ocean beaches.

"The battleground is Mildred-Ruth Lakes Lease No. 4, straddling the 57th parallel a scant 600 miles from the Arctic Circle. Here (Sun) is establishing the first commercial project to extract petroleum from the fabulous Athabasca oil sands."

Sun Magazine
Summer 1964

J. Howard Pew toured the
Athabasca plant in 1966.

Fort McMurray, Alberta, oil
sands plant in 1984
produced an average of
46,700 barrels a day of
synthetic crude oil.

In the early 1960s, Thayer, a senior vice
president of Sun, was on the point of retiring
when J. Howard Pew convinced him to stay on
and oversee the building of the oil sands plant.
Thayer eventually became the first president of
Great Canadian Oil Sands Limited.

Sun was the first to enter the oil sands. Others
have considered it, but in nearly two decades of
operation only one other plant, Syncrude, has
joined Sun with a venture of its own.

Between them they have turned a once quiet
little north woods outpost of 1,000 people into the
now-thriving city of Fort McMurray with upwards
of 35,000 citizens.

"J. Howard's philosophy was to be a pioneer and
get in there first," says Ken Heddon. "He knew
inflation was going to come and he knew oil was
going to become scarce and prices would go up.

"I guess you'd say he was about eight or 10
years early in his timing. But his vision was
certainly clear."

In 1965 Canadian Highways
Minister Gordon Taylor
(right) and GCOS Chairman
W. Harold Rea presided over
official opening of new
bridge over Athabasca River.

Some projects are a long time
aborning. Sun's Sarnia, Ontario,
refinery had a gestation period of
more than 20 years and involved a man with a
plan to build the perfect refinery.

Sun took the first major step toward building a
Canadian refinery in 1946 when J. Howard Pew
began negotiations to acquire a site on the Saint
Clair River northeast of Detroit.

The site offered preeminent advantages: direct
access to Great Lakes shipping routes; highway,
rail and pipeline transportation links throughout
Canada and into the U.S.; plentiful electricity from
the Ontario Hydro-Electric Power Commission;

abundant water for plant operations. It was the perfect site for the perfect plan.

The man with the plan was Clarence Thayer. In the 1920s, Thayer was a young engineer for a West Coast refiner who had been given an assignment to design a "model" refinery, one that could be operated easily and efficiently and laid out so it could be readily expanded into a larger facility.

By the time he joined Sun in 1926, Thayer had not yet been given the opportunity to build the model refinery he had designed, and wouldn't for the next 25 years. As Sun's manufacturing vice president, he was in charge of improvement projects at the Marcus Hook and Toledo refineries. The opportunity he had prepared for so long ago finally came in 1951, when Sun gave the go-ahead for the Sarnia refinery.

"Eighteen people and a plant manager started this refinery in 1953," says John Minardi, Sarnia's human resources manager.

In addition to its many technical innovations, Sarnia's personnel policies were also unique.

Organizational distinctions were minimized. There were no hourly workers; all employees were salaried. Important qualifications for hiring and advancement were desire and willingness to learn.

The refinery quickly became sought out by Canadians as a place to work. One employee, who had come to Canada from Poland to find a home for his family and a job with a future, had this to say when he was quoted for a magazine article 33 years ago: "Now I have found it. This is the answer to my dream."

It was a dream he shared with Clarence Thayer.

Clarence H. Thayer, manufacturing vice president, finally got his chance to build a model refinery when Sun built its Sarnia plant in the 1950s.

Oil industry mergers during the 1980s have become almost casual business news.

But they were a less common story back in 1968 when two petroleum giants announced that they had reached a friendly agreement to join forces through an exchange of shares.

The Sun/Sunray DX courtship began almost by chance. Robert G. Dunlop, president of Sun, and Paul Taliaferro, chairman of Tulsa-based DX, were seated next to each other at a 1967 industry dinner in Midland, Texas.

"I knew Paul Taliaferro only casually, but since they seated us alphabetically — Sun and Sunray — we got to talking and it seemed there might be an opportunity for us to put the companies together," recalls Dunlop.

Both companies began studying each other and the fit seemed like a smooth one with very few antitrust implications.

Sun operated mainly in the East and DX mainly in the Midwest. Sun was about twice the size of DX by almost every business measurement. The companies abutted, rather than overlapped, in almost all of their territorial marketing and refining regions.

From a business standpoint, a merger, with Sun being the surviving company, made all kinds of sense for both sides.

But the biggest concern of both Taliaferro and Dunlop was the possible impact on people. Even though DX had grown through the years by merger and acquisition, the merger with Sun was still an unsettling prospect to its people. For Sun, which had never done anything like this before, the people impact was even more traumatic.

"It took us a little longer than it should have, maybe," says Bob Dunlop. "We could have moved more quickly if we wanted to be unconcerned about people. But that's what appealed to me about Taliaferro. His concern was for people and he was a real gentleman."

Dale Stone, retired human resources senior vice president, a one-time DX employee and a member of the Sun/DX merger team, remembers the same concern.

"We took a year-and-a-half to study how best to put things together," he says. "There was no merger and no mergee. The employees in both organizations were going to have equal shots at the new jobs."

In the smoothest way possible, the two organizations started melding into each other — some 30,000 employees managing and operating more than $2 billion in assets out of which they would help form the new Sun organization.

W. C. (Bill) Whaley, former Sunray DX president, who had retired before the merger was considered, recalled that he felt good about DX merging with Sun.

"I was born and reared in the oil business and Sun was more considerate of its employees than any company I know of," he said.

In retrospect, there are those who would debate certain aspects of the merger.

John P. Neafsey, Sun's chief financial officer and former DX employee, expresses those thoughts when he suggests: "There's a balance to be struck between fairness and movement and I think this was over-balanced in the direction of being circumspect and fair."

Still, Neafsey says that at the time Sun needed to "shake up its hierarchical style of management" and that the changes for the good that have taken place in the company over the last decade could not have happened without an external catalyst such as the merger.

"So, from that standpoint, I think Sun was a great beneficiary."

In summary, Neafsey echoes the feelings of the overwhelming majority of Sun-connected people when he calls the merger "extraordinarily well planned and very humanely executed."

Addition of the DX brand expanded Sun's marketing territory beyond the Mississippi River.

The 1968 merger brought 85,000-barrel-a-day Tulsa, Okla., refinery into Sun.

"Lay the line in a direction northwest from Twin Oaks to a point near the town of Malvern, on the Pennsylvania Railroad. When you reach there, call me . . . "

— from J. Edgar Pew
to Frank L. Hadley
June 9, 1930

W ith that message, construction of America's first long-distance petroleum products pipeline began. When completed in 1931, the 730-mile system would have the capacity to move 18,000 barrels of gasoline from Sun's terminal at Twin Oaks, Pa., to Syracuse, N.Y., Cleveland, Ohio, and, through branch lines, to cities in between.

J. Edgar Pew, vice president of Sun, who oversaw the landmark project, remained the first president of Sun Pipe Line Company until his death in 1946. Direct responsibility for building the system fell on veteran pipeliner Frank Hadley.

There was nothing new in 1930 about pipelines. Almost since the beginning of the petroleum industry they had been used to transport natural gas and crude oil from producing fields to refineries. But in 1930, there were many who believed that moving gasoline under river bottoms and over mountain ranges was unnecessarily risky.

Two principal visions kept Sun from being

Sun pipeline emerges at Twin Oaks, Pa., pumping station to connect with pumps and storage tanks.

dissuaded: the economic advantages of pipelines and Sun's confidence in its ability to carry off the project. Those visions were kept alive despite America's plunge into the Great Depression and Sun's own declining fortunes (from $98 million in sales in 1930 to $69 million the following year).

The first motor fuel ever to reach the Great Lakes from the Atlantic coast by pipeline arrived in Cleveland on June 21, 1931. On August 19 pipeline shipments of motor fuel began to arrive at Syracuse from Marcus Hook.

The motor fuel was Blue Sunoco.

ollege never caught my interest. I was too anxious to get moving in the world," Sun director B. Ray Thompson, Sr., once told a reporter. Get moving he did. His start was a job as a helper in a family-owned Tennessee sawmill that happened to have a coal seam under it.

"I began mining to supply our lumbering operations. Then, as we developed excess production, I began to sell coal all over the South." That was in 1932.

From there, Thompson built one of the nation's largest privately owned coal companies. In 1979, his Elk River Resources, Inc., with its mining operations in Kentucky and Virginia and 186 million tons of coal reserves in those two states and West Virginia became part of Sun in a $300 million transaction.

The acquisition was Sun's second major venture into coal and its first east of the Mississippi. In 1976, Sun's Cordero mine near Gillette, Wyo., began producing surface-mined coal for sale to electric utilities.

Elk River gave Sun a strong sales base with major Eastern utilities in need of dependable delivery of high-quality, low-sulfur steam coal and steel companies in need of high-grade metallurgical and coking coal.

By 1983, production had grown by nearly 35 percent, while new acquisitions had expanded Elk River's reserves by more than 70 percent.

In the two decades prior to 1979, Thompson's company had been sought out by nearly a score of corporate suitors. Why did he finally sell to Sun?

"I liked what I saw," he said.

Elk River employees mine coal from underground and surface mines in Kentucky, Virginia and West Virginia.

Elk River produces coal for electric utilities along the Eastern Seaboard from Canada to Florida.

B. Ray Thompson, Sr., (left) . . . in the coal business for more than 50 years.

Robert G. Dunlop
President 1947-1970
Chairman 1970-1974

Bob Dunlop and U.S. space pioneer Wernher von Braun receiving honorary degrees in 1959. At right is Sun's executive director of R&E Chalmer Kirkbride.

Bob Dunlop took a temporary job in Sun's accounting department in the depths of the Great Depression.

It was 1933 and the bank holiday had cost him his accountant's position with a Philadelphia CPA firm.

"I was very depressed for about 24 hours," he remembers. "Then I started out to look for a job."

The Sun job became permanent and so did Bob Dunlop — 14 years later he was made president of Sun and now, 53 years later, he's still a member of its board.

The son of Scottish-born parents, Dunlop grew up in Collingswood, N.J., near Philadelphia. He won a scholarship to the prestigious Wharton School of Finance and Commerce at the University of Pennsylvania and then earned part of his expenses by shipping out on freighters during the summers.

Dunlop was only 37 when he was named to head Sun. In the next 27 years, first as president and then as chairman his last four years, he piled up an exceptional record of development and placed his own mark of achievement on Sun.

J. Howard Pew picked Dunlop to be his successor and personally groomed him for the job. Bob Dunlop had weathered the tests of working at Howard's elbow and even though he seemed very young for the job, in 1947 he was chosen as the first non-Pew in 60 years to head the Sun organization.

From the beginning Dunlop steered Sun with a dignity and personal charm that was to become his trademark. Stories of his visits to Sun facilities are legendary and he still prides himself on the number of Sun people he knows personally.

In the Dunlop years

. . . at 1953 christening of the *S.S. New Jersey Sun* with daughter Barbara, wife Brownie and son Richard.

... descending some 300 feet into underground storage facilities beneath Marcus Hook refinery. With Dunlop is vice president Clarence Thayer.

the company grew on every front. Revenues increased sixfold, profits ninefold and assets leaped into the billions. But his real and lasting mark on the company was registered in the broad strokes of his major projects:

■ The Venezuelan venture that led to Sun's rich Lake Maracaibo oil discovery in 1957.

■ The introduction of Custom Blending in gasoline marketing in 1958.

■ The $150 million, 66,000-barrel-a-day refinery complex in Yabucoa, Puerto Rico. Opened in 1971, the plant created jobs and income and did much to alleviate unemployment on the island.

■ The merger with Sunray DX Oil Company in 1968 — a bold stroke that was to turn Sun into a mammoth corporation and change the framework of the company forever.

These and scores of lesser corporate decisions mark Dunlop as an in-novator who kept Sun on the move, ever changing, ever developing, ever charting its own bold paths in an industry that thrives on change and bold ventures.

"At Sun it was my unique opportunity to bridge the old and the new," he says. "My period of service ranged from the days of direct executive control through the complete reorganization in the late '60s."

Though retired, Dunlop and his wife, Brownie — a former Sun employee — live near corporate headquarters and are familiar faces at Sun.

Dunlop maintains an office in the Sun building and regularly attends meetings of the board.

A birthday cake and its attendant well-wishers singing to Bob Dunlop in his office is a scene typical of the affectionate relationship he still has with the people of Sun.

... testifying before U.S. House Ways and Means Committee on petroleum tax policy in 1974.

The VenSun terminal on Lake Maracaibo was at Punta de Palmas on the Lake's western shore.

Remembers retired pipeliner J. Neill Fuquay:

"In the late '50s, I was part of the team that made a recommendation to Bob Dunlop and Jack Pew and some others about establishing a terminal down in Maracaibo, Venezuela. This was the first meeting at this level that I had ever participated in.

"We laid it out and I was expecting them to say, 'Well, thank you, and we'll consider this and in a month or two you might hear something and you might not.'

"But, when we got through, Bob Dunlop said, 'Well, that really sounds pretty good to me. Jack, what do you think?' Jack said, 'I believe that's the answer to what we need.'"

What Sun needed was low cost foreign crude to offset the competitive edge other oil companies were gaining at the gasoline pump from cheaper overseas sources.

The upshot was Sun's first large-scale production outside the United States — the Sun-led exploration and production complex tapping the rich reserves under Lake Maracaibo, Venezuela. Sun had looked into exploration possibilities in Venezuela in the 1920s, but it was this later venture that marked the real beginning of Sun as an international petroleum producer.

The first well came in on Nov. 29, 1957. The next decade saw nearly 100 producing wells, 450 million barrels of production (200 million of them being Sun's share) and development of one of the greatest exploration, production, crude gathering and natural gas fractionating complexes in the history of offshore oil.

For M.D. (Zeke) Noble, it was a once-in-a-lifetime career opportunity:

"I was young and Sun had difficulty interesting people in going to Venezuela. I had four very small children, but my family and I picked up and moved to Maracaibo. We lived in a house on a dirt street. But that experience was the highlight of my career," says the man who rose to lead Sun's international exploration efforts.

At the peak of production, there were seven flow stations in the Lake, gathering, testing and transporting crude oil taken from VenSun wells. Sun's operations in Lake Maracaibo continued until 1975, when Venezuela nationalized its oil industry.

Tankers waiting to dock at VenSun's terminal.

The $150 million complex Sun launched at Yabucoa, Puerto Rico, in 1969 included a 66,000-barrel-a-day refinery, an all-weather harbor for vessels of 50,000 deadweight tons and bigger, and jobs for more than 400 local residents in an economically depressed area.

Puerto Rico needed industrial development to dent chronically high unemployment. For approved projects that generated jobs, the island was excepted from then-existing U.S. restrictions on imports of foreign crude and unfinished oils.

Recalls W. J. (Wib) Magers, who was in charge of the Yabucoa project, which he calls the most interesting job he ever had: "It took four years of negotiations to resolve the questions related to quotas and other issues."

In that time, costs for the refinery kept escalating and profit potential kept dimming, but Sun continued on.

Reason: The Puerto Rico refinery was not only a commercial venture. It had the added social purpose of boosting employment and serving the island's economic development.

Sun stayed with it until it did.

Sun Chairman Robert G. Dunlop (left) and Puerto Rico Sun President W. J. (Wib) Magers (right) participated in 1969 groundbreaking.

With Lake Maracaibo behind it, in 1960 Sun ventured into deeper international waters, collaborating in geophysical studies of the North Sea.

From that small beginning, Sun was to explore for and develop production in one of the harshest environments on the offshore world oil frontier.

In 1965, Sun established, in London, North Sea Sun Oil Company Ltd. to manage its expanding activities in the United Kingdom. The following year, as a member of the Arpet group of companies, North Sea Sun joined in the discovery of the productive Hewett gas field off Britain's southeast coast.

By the early 1970s, Sun was looking to the north part of the sea. What were once considered marginal prospects because of high exploration and production costs were being made more economically promising by rising world crude oil prices and advancing deep sea drilling technology.

Sun's first probe of the North Sea's remote northern basin was aborted at a depth of 9,700 feet when the exploration rig, damaged by heavy seas, had to be towed some 150 miles to Edinburgh, Scotland, for repair.

Subsequent results were better: 1975 saw the discovery and later confirmation of hydrocarbons on a block between Scotland and Norway, later to become part of Sun's Balmoral field. In 1980, Sun gained interests in more offshore blocks through the $35 million acquisition of Viking Oil Limited. Discovery of the Glamis field just southwest of Balmoral came in 1983.

Bob McClements, Sun president and CEO, sees Sun's North Sea activities as "one more significant step in the company's continuing search for oil and gas. It is part of our strategy of reinforcing our base as a supplier of energy."

Sun expects the initial production rate from its North Sea Balmoral field to reach 35,000 barrels a day.

Sun's Balmoral field is located 140 miles off the northeast coast of Scotland in 470 feet of water.

In the stormy North Sea, Sun in 1980 began exploratory drilling on the block acquired with the purchase of Viking Oil Limited.

Rig *Constellation* made a major North Sea discovery, opening Hewett gas field.

Settling toward its home on the floor of the North Sea is 840-ton template through which production wells in Balmoral field are drilled.

In 1982, Sun turned its attention to another new oil frontier: the People's Republic of China, which that year issued invitations to oil companies around the world in its search for partners to help find and develop oil off its 3,000-mile-long coastline.

Sun wasn't a complete stranger to China in 1982. In the 1920s and '30s, Sunoco oils and greases were distributed there and elsewhere in the Orient from an office in the port of Shanghai.

Sun waited for more than a year for word on its exploration bid. When the answer came, it was "yes." In late 1983, Sun, along with other international companies, was granted shares in exploration tracts in the South China Sea and the Gulf of Beibu (formerly the Gulf of Tonkin).

In early 1984, a Sun-operated jack-up rig was towed to its position off Hainan Island in the Gulf of Beibu, and drilling began.

Exploring isn't Sun's only current China connection. Sunoco oils are once again being distributed there, this time from a new lube oil blending and packaging plant in the port city of Shekou. The $6 million facility is another joint venture between Sun and the Chinese government.

This is how Robert P. Hauptfuhrer, president of Sun Exploration and Production Company, looks upon Sun's China involvement:

"We're out there on what I like to call the frontier of Sun's future. The fact that there's much more oil and gas yet to be found overseas than in the United States has brought us to China. It's also taken us to France, England, Sudan, Colombia. And we're considering many other areas."

In China's Gulf of Beibu Sun is the operator of a 206-square-mile tract.

Sun trademarks of 1920s and '30s were familiar to people in the Far East.

Nationalist Chinese soldiers in 1929 in front of their barracks near Shanghai with containers of Sun oils.

Sun engineers helped train Chinese drilling crews.

Four million new acres to explore came to Sun with 1980 purchase of Texas Pacific properties.

Sun Chairman Ted Burtis calls it "the biggest decision I was involved in. It was a swallow-hard-and-go-ahead kind of thing." An impressive acknowledgement, considering Burtis' business career spans more than four decades.

The big decision he refers to is Sun's 1980 acquisition of the U.S. oil and gas properties of Seagram Company's Texas Pacific Oil Company. The scope of that venture gives some clue as to why it might be especially memorable.

- It was a $2.3 billion deal, at that time the second largest acquisition in the history of U.S. business.
- It brought to Sun some 123 million barrels of crude oil and 315 billion cubic feet of natural gas in proved hydrocarbon reserves.
- On a daily basis, Sun picked up current production totaling 32,000 barrels of oil and 104 million cubic feet of gas, boosting its daily output to 188,000 barrels of oil and 1,117 million cubic feet of gas.
- The exploratory properties Sun acquired doubled the company's unexplored lands in the U.S. to nearly eight million acres.
- It had all the cloak-and-dagger secrecy of a spy thriller . . . it even had a code name — "Tomahawk."

From January 1980, when Ted Burtis was first approached about Sun's interest in buying the TP properties, to Sept. 12, 1980, when the deal was finally set, several dozen Sun people from corporate headquarters in Radnor and exploration and production offices in Dallas worked carefully and sometimes clandestinely on Project Tomahawk.

There were reserve numbers to be analyzed. Economic evaluations to be made. Production and income figures to be studied. Future oil prices and taxes to be predicted. A legal structure to be created. All aimed at arriving at a fair and reasonable purchase price . . . and one that would get Sun the prize.

Early in the delicate negotiations, Sun wasn't the only suitor TP had and that accounted for the circumspect demeanor on the part of the Tomahawk team.

"We took the position that the only way to do it was to be pre-emptive and make the game be played the way we wanted to play it and not the way the seller wanted to play it. And it worked," says Ted Burtis.

Bob Hauptfuhrer agrees. "Other potential acquirers had deeper pocketbooks than we did,"

New exploration
opportunities included
acreage in Wyoming's
Bridger Mountains.

In Western Overthrust Belt
drilling crews search for oil
atop Wyoming's Prater
Mountain, living on site for
weeks at a time.

says the president of Sun Exploration and Production Company. "So we had to sift through and figure out what our competitive advantage might be. We decided we had to be early, prepared and able to act quickly."

Executive Vice President Gordon Hillhouse recalled that during a particularly sensitive time in the negotiations Sun managed to prevent information leaks by preparing briefing papers only hours before they were needed.

"We did not intend to get into a bidding contest," Hillhouse said.

Not every moment of the nine months it took to finalize the deal was worry-free, but in the end Sun prevailed.

"We had astounding good luck," believes Gordon Hillhouse. "Everything we counted on came about."

Texas Pacific was a significant event in Sun's

history for a number of reasons, not the least being that it announced Sun's determination to place renewed emphasis on developing domestic oil and gas reserves.

Ted Burtis views the TP acquisition as a watershed in Sun's back-to-basics energy strategy. He also credits the move with having a profound impact on "what was perceived as being okay behavior" in the company.

"The TP acquisition did a couple of things," he says. "It demonstrated that, yes, we can take a bold step. We are willing to use our debt capacity. And that it's okay to think in pretty unconventional ways."

Senior vice president Jack Neafsey agrees, saying: "Texas Pacific was important not so much for what it was as an investment but because it forced the company to really embrace change with a vengeance."

Indeed, the Texas Pacific acquisition did much to convince the outside world that Sun was serious about getting back on the energy track.

"We had come to that point of redirection where we had to define where we were going and how we were going to get there," says Ted Burtis. "If there was one strong signal that we meant what we said about staying in the energy business, TP was it."

At TP's Ranger Field, Sun is using injection systems to force trapped hydrocarbons out of decades-old wells.

Texas Pacific was an early comer to the Western Overthrust Belt, one of the most promising — and challenging — geological formations in the world.

At Exeter, Sun's strategy from the outset was to increase production quickly and efficiently.

A T-shirt sold by a travel agency in Taft, Calif., says "Ski Taft." It shows a skier plummeting down the vertical wooden legs of an oil derrick.

Which is a local joke because there are no big hills in Taft and it never snows there. But this community on the western fringe of the San Joaquin Valley north of Los Angeles has other things: One of them is heavy oil, lots of it.

Sun had been buying California heavy oil for years before its 1968 merger with Sunray DX Oil Company gave Sun a direct stake in the Midway-Sunset field just north of Taft.

That stake increased considerably in 1984 when Sun acquired independently owned Exeter Oil Company for $76 million and the nearby pro-

The Exeter and Victory acquisitions gave Sun prime production properties in two California oil fields.

ducing properties of the Victory Oil Company for $281 million.

"The acquisitions reflect Sun's strategy of acquiring existing producing properties and, using its production know-how, quickly bringing them up to snuff," Sun President and CEO Bob McClements said at the time.

What the two acquisitions gave Sun were more than 100 million barrels of proved domestic crude oil reserves.

What the Sun engineers in charge of the projects got was the opportunity to live up to Sun's strong reputation in utilizing enhanced recovery technology to get more oil out.

As drilling rigs worked 24 hours a day, trucks rolled in off State Highway 33 all winter and spring, raising clouds of dust as they brought in components for the new oil/water separating system, the large, 50-million Btu electric generators, the air pollution control system, production pumps and flow lines.

Exeter production, which hovered at about 450

Work crews began operating in the Exeter fields as soon as the purchase was final.

to 500 barrels a day when Sun took over in January 1984, soon became 600 barrels, then 700, 800, 900, 1,000 and kept going.

With Exeter under its belt by mid-summer, the Sun engineering team moved on to Victory. Drilling rigs began biting into the earth of the larger field, trucks moved in the equipment, the new facilities rose and so did production.

Late one afternoon in the summer of '84, Jack Hiatt, who was then production superintendent, stood on a hill, surveying what had been accomplished at Exeter in such a short time.

In his more than 40 years there, Hiatt had seen production at Midway-Sunset grow, then decline until resuscitated by the introduction of steam injection in the 1960s, and now spiral again.

"I'm very proud of what we've done here," he said. "Of course, it takes good people to accomplish all we've been able to. The whole thing is people. They're what make a company."

Sun's experience producing heavy oil by steam injection boosted Exeter production from 500 to 6,400 barrels a day in two years.

"It doesn't matter where in the company you work; what you find is first-class people trying to do a good job. They want to be a part of Sun's success."

Robert H. Campbell—1985

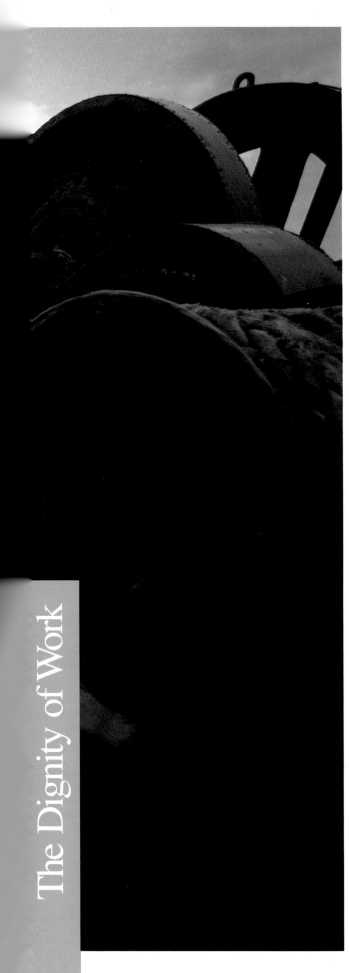

To the many thousands of people who have worked at Sun during its first century, the company has brought meaning as well as money.

For some, the excitement was in being part of the adventures in the oil patch. For others, Sun meant the steady satisfaction of a career in a major industry. For many, the best of Sun was the pleasure of the company of other Sun people.

Asked to describe what Sun means to them, many people who have worn the label "Sun employee" talk about the "people," the "closeness" and the "family feeling" that gives working life at Sun an extra measure of fulfillment.

"I've made a lot of permanent friends in all of the Sun locations where I've worked. I consider those people part of my family and part of my life," says Nell Short Clark, executive secretary at Sun Marine Terminals in Nederland, Texas.

Charles Heidrick, retired production attorney, agrees. "Whether it's a celebration or an employee outing, sickness or difficult times, we're just a real unusual company that shows a warm feeling for the troops," he says.

Some employees mentioned "security" as an important element of their Sun working life. Although, for younger workers at least, that doesn't appear to be an overriding concern.

Nell Short Clark
Sun Marine Terminals

"After I graduated, Sun trained me and got me right on-line working on some very important projects. They stake a lot in employees and their ideas. That makes an employee feel important."
Bob Hartland
Geophysicist
Dallas

Charles Heidrick
Retiree

"Younger employees today generally do not seek security," says Joseph Colella, a crude oil trader at Sun Oil Trading Company. "We seek opportunity."

Many other Sun people appreciated the company's "integrity," the "freedom" given to employees to learn and grow, the "opportunity" for advancement and the "confidence and energy" which is an integral part of the company.

Words such as these underscore Sun's outstanding reputation as a place to work. Those words — and the feelings that inspire them — are the tangible expressions of the special fondness with which so many Sun employees regard their days at Sun.

"Our dedication to Sun was recognized and rewarded. That's why we fell in love with the company and gave 100 percent in return," says Walter Erwin, a retired Sun geologist in Dallas.

"I'm afraid that we took things for granted that we shouldn't have. The longer you're away, the more you realize the wonderful aspects of it," observes Dick Rohrer, retired from the Marcus Hook refinery's personnel department.

Sometimes that loyalty toward Sun stirred the first day on the job.

Harry Crawford, retired district marketing manager, shares a moment from his early days at Sun in 1927.

"I was working at the Marcus Hook refinery and an older worker commented, 'You're new here.' I told him I had just started. He said, 'Well, son, I think you made a wonderful choice. You can look and look and look but you'll never find a company with a heart as big as Sun.'"

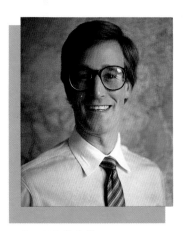

Joseph Colella
Sun Oil Trading Company

Over the years, working at Sun has often been a family endeavor. Two examples: In 1948 eight members of the Marshall family (left) were employed at the Marcus Hook refinery. In 1985 six members of the Carter clan enjoy an association with the Toledo refinery.

Cecil Colville was fresh out of Southern Methodist University and had never seen an oil field, when he reported to work at Sun's East Texas oil fields in 1936.

"The fellow in charge asked me if I had ever climbed a derrick before," relates the retired production manager. "I told him that I hadn't and he said, 'Well, don't hurry. I'm not going to holler

The oil patch then and now. Arkansas' Smackover oil field in the '20s (bottom). The Hitts Lake, Texas, field in the '80s.

at you. Just take your time.' Over the years, I came to recognize that helpful attitude as typical of Sun employees."

The atmosphere has been one of a closeknit family, where the mutual care and concern was evident in good times and bad. People worked hard and they worked together.

Retiree Orla (Moe) Bowhall started in the marine department in 1928. He says that "we used to fight and argue, but when the chips were down, we were all for the company."

"Sun was really a family company," believes retiree John Kriebel who went to work at the Marcus Hook refinery in 1925, right out of high school.

"People worked together as a team," he continues. "I can't remember anyone leaving the office when a colleague had too much unfinished work to go home on time. We all pitched in and we all left together."

Greg Driscoll, special fuels sales manager in Sun Refining and Marketing Company, thinks that this spirit of helping one another is part of the reason for Sun's success. "The cooperative attitude here makes me comfortable," he says. "No one knows it all, but all of us know it together."

**Greg Driscoll
Sun Refining and Marketing
Company**

"Sun is a good company . . . and a good company to work for. Sun gives a lot to the community in education, culture, sports, health and welfare. I'm pleased to be part of that."

**Jose Lopez
Community Coordinator
Puerto Rico Refinery**

Testing engine performance at Marcus Hook auto lab.

"I've been with Sun for five years. I think the best part of my job is getting to work with people from different parts of the company."

**Elverez Allen
Account Supervisor
Tulsa Credit Card Center**

H. Robert Sharbaugh
President 1970-1976
Chairman 1975-1979

Bob Sharbaugh made sweeping organizational changes at Sun during the 1970s. He was positioning the company to meet the times; he was building flexibility into its operations, and he was always, in his words, "seeking the competitive advantage."

Perhaps most of all, he was teaching Sun people that they had potential to grow, to expand their own horizons, to contribute more to the Sun organization than the narrow confines of their job descriptions would indicate.

Bob Sharbaugh was still a scholarship chemical engineering student at Carnegie-Mellon and only 17 when he came to work in the Marcus Hook refinery in the summer of 1946.

He returned to Sun full time after graduation in 1948 and worked his way up through the refinery management team over the next 12 years.

Eventually he was slotted in as assistant to the refining vice president. It was from this spot that

Bob Sharbaugh receiving award in 1973 for his many contributions to youth.

Bob Sharbaugh made the leap to the presidency of Sun. After 22 years in the company, he was still just 41 years old when he was made president.

It was 1970. The Sun merger with Sunray DX had taken place recently and the two companies were still trying to get the hang of operating as one. The petroleum industry was looking at the prospect of weakening prices, diminishing reserves and heavy environmental and governmental pressures.

For the next several years after Sharbaugh took the reins, Sun went through a rapid series of organizational realignments. The emphasis was on pushing managerial responsibility further down in the organization and freeing up the executive suite for more forward-planning responsibilities. Other steps followed:
- Sun's headquarters were moved out of downtown Philadelphia to the suburb of St. Davids, thus separating corporate staff from operations.
- Emphasis was placed on raising the cash dividend and pushing up the stock price.

... with former Philadelphia mayor Frank Rizzo (left) on offshore drilling platform in the Atlantic Ocean.

■ The board of directors expanded its membership, naming the first outsider, former U.N. Ambassador William Scranton, and the first woman, Mary Wells Lawrence.

■ A management training school was founded and individual employees were made responsible for their own career advancement.

By 1974 Bob Sharbaugh had taken on the additional role of chief executive and the next year he was also named chairman of the board.

In the fall of 1975, Sharbaugh announced to New York security analysts that he was restructuring the company into 14 decentralized operating units, a non-operating parent company and two property companies. Each unit would have its own president and would become its own profit center.

The next year Sharbaugh received enough shareholder votes to change the name of the company to Sun Company, Inc. (dropping the word "oil") to reflect more closely Sun's involvement in other businesses.

By 1978, it became obvious that Sharbaugh's vision for the direction of the company was differing widely from the majority position on Sun's board — particularly after the Sharbaugh administration bought heavily into Becton, Dickinson and Company, a medical supply firm.

So Bob Sharbaugh began preparations to leave the corporation after 30 years of service. After leaving Sun, he set up his own consulting business, accepting directorships in several major corporations.

"My affection for the people of Sun will last forever," he says. "In many ways a part of me will always be there. It was an exciting experience and I'm glad I did it."

... at 1971 annual meeting of Sun shareholders.

In the southwest during the 1930s Jack Pew set the pace. Jack was J. Edgar Pew's son, and in charge of production. He expected Sun people to work hard, come in early and stay late, and he rewarded them for their efforts.

"You'd come into the parking lot at 6:30 in the morning and it would be half full. You'd go out at 6:00 at night and it still would be half full. Those were hours that you couldn't put a dollar sign to," says Kingsley Schroeder, retired production vice president.

Tom Hill, who worked for the company for 41 years, retiring as manager of the southwest production division, notes that Sun people were always willing to do what was necessary to get the job done. "I don't care if it was Saturday or Sunday, if something arose, you'd give them a call and they'd come running to help," he says.

At one time, J. Howard Pew knew virtually every employee who worked at the Marcus Hook refinery. At the time of the plant's 50th anniversary in 1951, William G. Rhyder, one of the first employees hired at the refinery, remembered:

"That was one thing about J. Howard. Any time you had to go into a tank or down in the bottom of a ship, he would go with you. You couldn't tell to look at him that he was the boss, but you sure knew it if you worked for him. He worked hard himself and that's how he could always get a good day's work out of his men."

"Last year we achieved the best safety record in our group. Lost times injuries equalled a big zero. It was an attitude of commitment."

Ken McKeller
Loss Prevention Supervisor
Sarnia Refinery

"People here are willing to work and they want to improve themselves," said a citizen of Yabucoa, Puerto Rico, when Sun's refinery was being built there in the late 1960s. Some 400 people now work at the refinery.

The dedication of generations of employees has contributed greatly to Sun's success. Throughout his Sun career, Jack Pew helped foster that spirit and sense of caring.

Jack Pew

Drilling for oil in California's Exeter field.

"In the '20s, roustabouts worked seven days a week. The work day began at 7 a.m. and ended at 5 p.m. with a one-hour lunch break. Roustabout pay was 50¢ an hour for the nine hour work day."

Joe Owens
Retiree

I n the years following World War II, the idea that things would get better and better became a reality. America was growing and so was Sun. Refinery, pipeline and marketing operations all expanded.

"Buying new locations, building new service stations, promoting new products was a seven-day-a-week job. It was challenging and fun," says Harlan Snider, senior vice president of planning and public affairs who started his career in the marketing organization.

Working at Sun in the 1950s became more decentralized and diverse. Gradually, too, employees sought a bigger role in directing their own careers.

The 1968 merger of Sun and Sunray DX created a new company with new management and leadership. The task at hand was to merge two corporate cultures to create a third culture for a new organization.

"Paramount in the development of a new culture were feelings about people who need the freedom to take charge of their careers," says Dale Stone, retired human resources senior vice president.

Sun adopted principles governing human relationships that preserved the beliefs that traditionally characterized Sun and its employees.

At the same time, the company searched for ways to be responsive to a rapidly changing world. Pressured by political uncertainties, rapid technological advancement and energy shortages, the petroleum business was no longer predictable.

**Loading tank cars at the
Marcus Hook refinery.**

So Sun and its employees began to forge a new
— perhaps more mature — relationship.

"In a sense, the psychological contract that said
employees had a job for life at Sun was broken.
The new contract opened up opportunities for
people to develop themselves fully and to climb in
the organization," says Dale Stone.

Some employees missed the old days; others
welcomed the change.

*"I've worked here 11 years
and I'm the first of three
woman hired for an operator's
job. I'm proud to come here
to work, that's why I've
stayed. I like working in a
man's world."*

**Avundia (Wanda) Rodriguez
Operator
Toledo Refinery**

Tom Deal and Marcia Faykus of Dallas' legal group.

Mending fences at Big Horn
Ranch, Sun's cattle ranch
and reclamation research
center, near the Cordero
coal mine in Gillette, Wyo.

"I like being able to set goals and make things happen," says Roy J. Hodgen, area sales manager, Aviation and Wholesale Marketing, Sun Refining and Marketing Company. "Today the mentality of staying in a job until retirement doesn't exist. People like to think for themselves, assess an opportunity."

Sun offers multiple options. Employees can bid on jobs through an Internal Placement System, participate in the educational assistance program,

take advantage of career counselling services.

"I bid on a job in fuels in 1977 and on a managerial job in 1981," says Refining and Marketing's Greg Driscoll. "I landed both of them. Then I started an MBA program at the University of Pennsylvania. Sun paid nearly all of the bill."

Tom Tryon, a computer operator at Sun's Tulsa

From Kentucky coal mine to
Canadian refinery, Sun
employees pursue a variety
of energy challenges.

Sue Haldeman
Sun Oil Trading Company

Credit Card Center, got his degree in chemistry from the University of Tulsa and then went to work on a second degree, thanks to what he calls "the company's commitment to me to help me better myself."

"I'm impressed that at Sun we can do our own career planning, sign up for courses and get support and encouragement along the way," says Sue Haldeman, crude oil trader, Sun Oil Trading Company.

The things Sun did to unleash the talent and capability of employees and to identify able managers in the ranks were in keeping with

"When I started with Sun, I had no experience in the oil industry. Sun provided me with excellent training. Now, I have interesting projects to work on . . . Sun has let me grow professionally."

Alice Cameron
Geologist
Longview, Texas

employees' expectations of more flexibility and freedom. And they put Sun on the leading edge of human resources practices.

"Sun was the first company in the oil industry to open up the job-bidding system and to introduce outplacement counselling when we first needed to reduce complement," says Bill Rutherford, human resources senior vice president. "Helping people use their talent more fully and make their own decisions carries on the Sun tradition of caring about people."

From Longview, Texas, to Toledo, Ohio . . . from Philadelphia to Tokyo . . . employees acknowledge the opportunity to share their professional time and talents with Sun.

The company returns the compliment.

"Our people work hard," says Bob McClements, president and CEO. "The issue is not motivating our people. The issue is leadership. Point our folks in a direction and they go. The challenge to all of us is to make sure they are pointed in the right direction."

The Value of Tradition

". . . the character of this company has been shaped by a century of integrity, loyalty and growth. It is a philosophy that puts care for human dignity and national liberty at the head of the list."

Theodore A. Burtis—1982

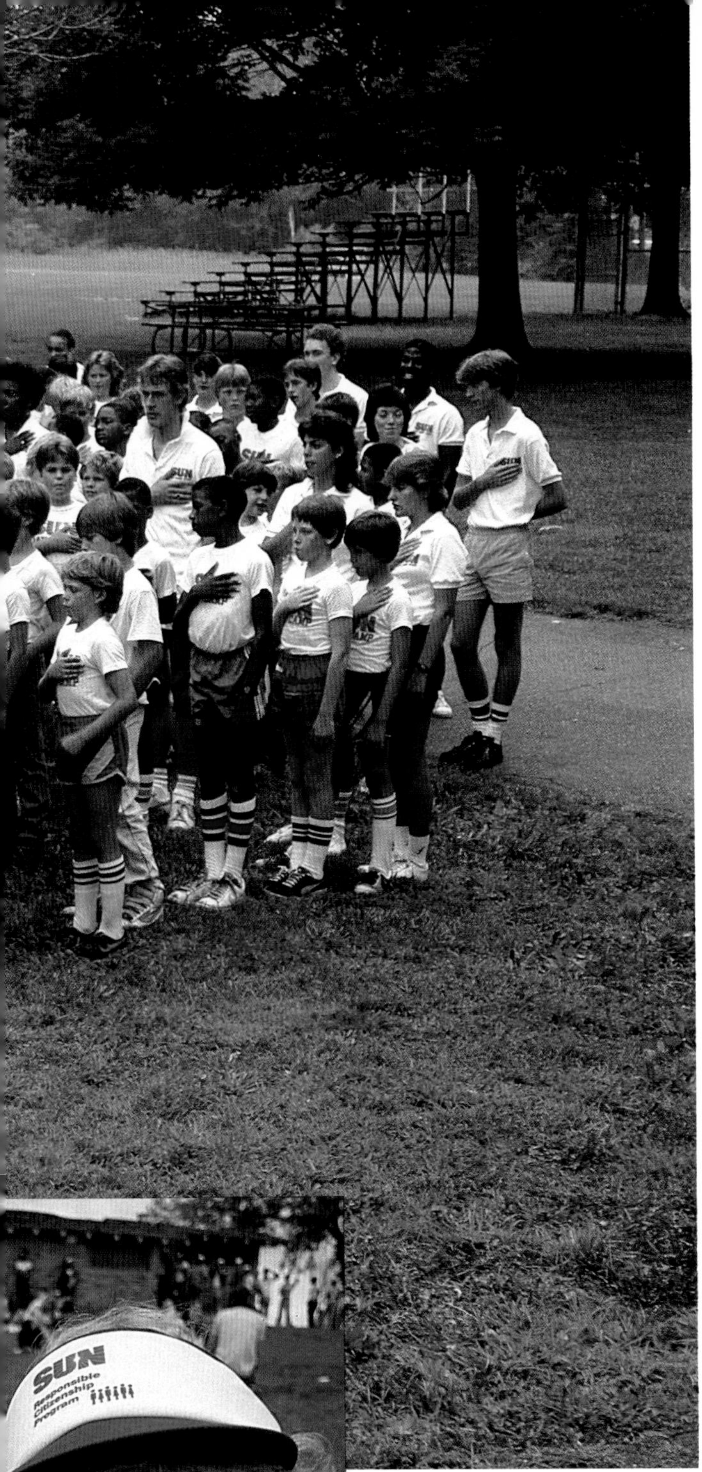

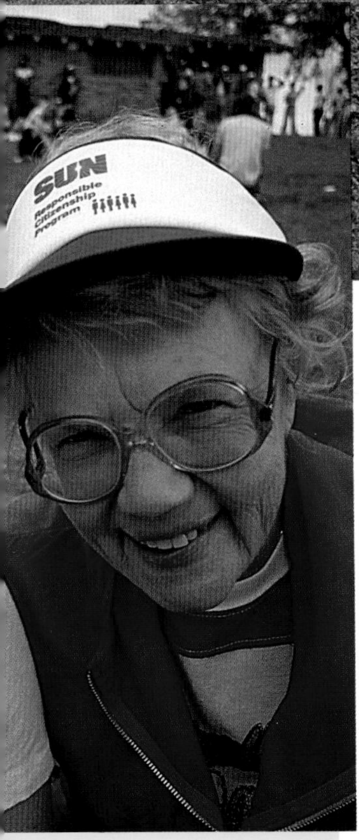

Over the years Sun Company has kept alive a rare spirit of personal respect and friendly cooperation. From that atmosphere has emerged a certain Sun style — a style not complicated nor pretentious. Sun is more dignified than flamboyant. More steady than surging. More conscientious than cutthroat. More successful than not.

To a large extent, Sun is the way the Pews were. More than just investors or entrepreneurs, they were business leaders. Because the Pews stayed actively engaged in Sun management for eight decades, the company's character was infused with their values. Those values stressed integrity, respect for others, loyalty, incentive, individual ingenuity, community and national responsibility.

That spirit affected the way Sun treated its employees, conducted its negotiations, operated its daily business and interacted with people and events outside the corporation. Eventually, that way of doing things became formalized in a creed, a set of principles which have long characterized the Sun organization.

In some ways the culture of Sun's earlier days has changed. The challenges to the oil industry in the 1980s have disturbed the cozy equanimity of a berth at Sun. Some of the warm touches of the early Sun culture in fact were possible because the times were generous.

In the 1980s, energy is still an immense industry. But its future belongs to the quick and the strong. At all energy companies this has brought changes: fewer employees and shifting organizational structures.

Even as this resettling takes place, a certain familiar feeling persists. The feeling that Sun is an excellent place to work. That here people of quality and caring pursue energy challenges. That being part of a company that conducts its business

Baseball team coach Rich Merchant, Sun Refining and Marketing Company.

with integrity is a legitimate source of pride. It's a pride deep enough to share — and Sun people do.

Vincent Verdiani, retired president of Sun Oil Trading Company, started Sun's crude oil trading function in 1974. "Going into the trading business was an adventuresome step," he says. "But the company trusted me and they let me do my own thing. Sun permitted its people to be different."

"All in all, I think people were happy with their careers," says Elmer Bradley, retired marketing vice president. "They were happy to have the opportunity to be part of Sun."

Sun and its employees also continue to demonstrate a well-tuned sense of responsibility to the larger world. For 100 years, the people of Sun Company have done more than just provide energy to a growing world. They have provided an example of how citizenship works. In the nation's capital and in the local town meeting, at the hospital and the high school, Sun people contribute their time, talent and money to improving conditions in the neighborhoods and the nation.

About the future shape of the business not even the best guessers will speculate with confidence. But, says director and retired Chairman Robert G. Dunlop, "I suspect the energy industry in 25, even 10 years is going to be significantly different than it is today."

To enjoy a future as privileged as the past, Sun will have to attend carefully to the present and look confidently to the future. For that task Sun will do well to know itself. Here, then, is a brief look at the way Sun is in some spheres. A way, not coincidentally, that has worked admirably for a century.

Sun employees who belong to the Marcus Hook, Pa., volunteer fire department.

Theodore A. Burtis
President 1976-1981
Chairman 1979-

With the election of Ted Burtis in 1976 Sun Company broke with its 93-year-old tradition of naming exceptionally young presidents.

Burtis was 55 — but he had been only 34 when he was named president and chairman of Houdry Process Corporation. So he had already had his turn as a young chief executive.

Another consideration was that Sun presidents had always grown up with the company.

Ted Burtis, on the other hand, had been at Sun only nine years.

In many ways, though, his years at Houdry put Burtis in close contact with Sun. Houdry was a onetime spin-off company that had its roots in Sun since the 1930s.

Burtis stepped down at Houdry and "walked down the street to Sun" (with a 20 percent cut in pay) in his mid-40s because he says he was looking for a new career with upward potential.

"At 45, I figured I had time to make a mistake, if I was going to, and still recover from it," he says. "I knew the people at Sun, I knew something about the business — it seemed like a good move."

The chemical engineer-

Ted Burtis receiving thanks of United Way representative for guiding the 1984 Southeastern Pennsylvania drive to a record fundraising achievement.

. . . with wife Billie at United Nations Concert and Ball. Burtis was 1984 national U.N. Day chairman.

ing graduate of Carnegie-Mellon and Texas A&M started as director of commercial development, and quickly moved up through the executive ranks at Sun. It was a scant two years after being named president that Burtis took on the

additional duties of chief executive. Six months later he became chairman.

In this position he began returning Sun to its historic and basic role as a developer and producer of energy resources. Sun's corporate strategy, which had become somewhat blurred in the early 1970s, was now brought back into sharp focus: Sun was reemphasizing the energy business and was backing its strategy with some bold Burtis decisions:

■ In 1979, Sun paid $300 million in stock for Elk River Resources, a large Eastern coal mining company.

■ In 1980, all the domestic oil and gas properties of Texas Pacific Oil Company were bought by Sun for $2.3 billion.

■ In 1982, Sun sold Sun Ship, a large shipbuilding facility which had been in the Sun family of companies since World War I.

■ Other companies, such as Sperry Sun, TOTE — other facilities, such as the Corpus Christi, Texas, and Duncan, Okla., refineries — were sold off.

"Once you settle on a strategic direction, then you must back up that choice with your actions," Burtis says.

As he restructured the company and swung it back to doing what it does best, Ted Burtis was gaining a reputation for being action-oriented and decisive.

At the same time, he was getting to be known as a chief executive with quiet charisma. Employees liked him and they liked dealing with him.

Though he is still chairman of the board, Burtis

. . . sailing off Avalon, N.J., with son Ted, Jr., one of three Burtis children.

stepped aside from the chief executive's position in 1985, noting that he had been at the helm of the company for seven years and "the time has come to pass the baton."

As chairman, Burtis is still at his desk and continuing to play an active role in Sun's relationships with governmental, business and community groups.

. . . hosting senior naval officers from 35 countries, visiting Sun for a business and energy briefing.

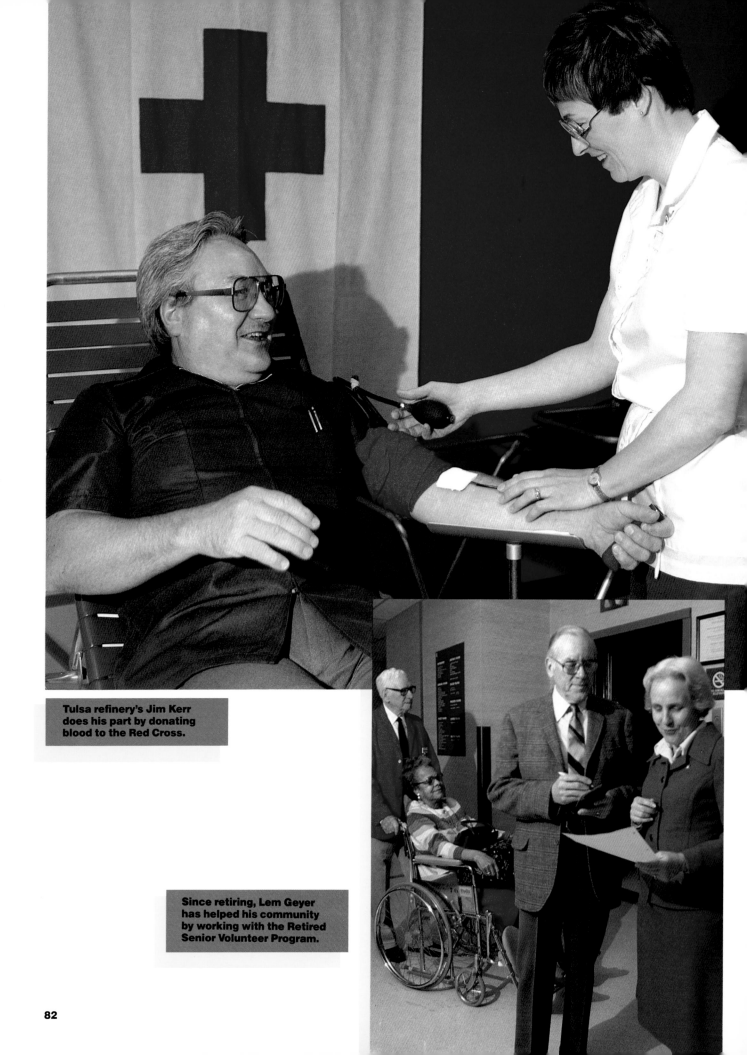

Tulsa refinery's Jim Kerr does his part by donating blood to the Red Cross.

Since retiring, Lem Geyer has helped his community by working with the Retired Senior Volunteer Program.

W hen Darwin and Patricia Ferguson moved to Jackson, Mich., they didn't know anyone in town. Mr. Ferguson had just started there as Sun's new district marketing manager. Mrs. Ferguson was beginning to set up the home. Both were about to discover just how friendly Sun people can be.

Soon after arriving, Mrs. Ferguson became critically ill. Rushed to the hospital, she lost a baby and nearly lost her life, too. What happened then still leaves her a touch awed — even now, 30 years later.

"Nobody even knew me, but everybody in the company went to the hospital and gave blood for me — without being asked," she says.

The Ferguson's new Sun friends were generous in other ways as well. It seems that daughter Patty turned three while Mrs. Ferguson was in the hospital. When the Sun warehouse manager found out about that, he and his wife came out to the Ferguson house and put on a party — complete with treats and presents — for Patty's birthday.

Extraordinary? Yes. Uncommon? No.

"The one thing we learned over the years was that we have a superior type of person working at Sun," says Darwin Ferguson, who retired in 1975 as executive vice president and director.

It's no secret that Sun people often share an almost family feeling. One reason for that may be that from the start Sun people have been appreciated by their employer.

"I think everybody was considered important by the company," observes Warren Burch, retired senior vice president of Sun Refining and Marketing Company. By the nature of wages and benefits, he believes that Sun is "possibly tops in the business."

The feeling that people came before profits stirred gratitude and good feelings toward Sun among generations of employees. Enjoying the hospitality, many have spent their entire working lives at Sun.

Kenneth F. Heddon, retired chairman of Sun's Canadian subsidiary, is one of those. "I never regretted my 39 years with Sun," he says firmly. "I had some opportunities to leave — at very substantial increases in salary. But I decided to stay with Sun because I liked the people and I liked the company."

So did Arch Ballou. He stayed 46 years, retiring as director of conservation and environmental affairs in the southwest. "For my first 30 years, it was unusual for anyone to leave," he remembers.

In fact, a saying went around that if you got a job at Sun, you had a job for life. Sun did offer its people a longevity that was perhaps unique.

But Chairman Ted Burtis points out that, as is so often the case, this particular corporate memory may have been burnished just a bit by time.

"The old thing about nobody ever leaving just isn't true," he says. "People came and went just like everywhere else.

"It's just that when Sun was a proprietorship, and particularly during the Depression, it was possible to subordinate earnings and keep people on. There wasn't the same kind of bottom line orientation that we have now," Burtis explains.

Robert W. Donahue, who served as vice chairman of the company, saw in Sun a forward-thinking employer. "J. Howard treated his people very humanely and was really ahead of his time in many ways," he says.

There are stories that J. Howard Pew visited employees who were in the hospital. That J. Edgar Pew would invite new employees into his office for a chat. That his son Jack Pew was constantly lending money to his people. And that if Bob Dunlop met you, he never forgot your name.

Retiree Cecil Colville observes that Sun was a supportive, attentive employer even as it grew larger. He tells of how Jack Pew, when he was in Dallas as assistant to the production vice president, insisted that his managers go out in the oil fields and talk to each of the workers once a year.

"Let them know you know they are there," was Jack Pew's instruction. For some area managers that meant shaking hands with 1,500 workers

from Florida to the Mexican border.

A spirit of partnership developed between employees and the company's management. The partnership became formalized in 1926 when Sun became one of the first companies in the nation to offer a stock purchase plan for employees.

The motivation, recalls Ted Burtis, was that "management thought it would be good for the company and good for the employees if employees had an ownership interest."

As the industry changes, the Sun style keeps evolving. Of necessity, says Robert H. Campbell, president of Sun Refining and Marketing Company.

"Any company that doesn't recognize the competitiveness of today's world will not be around for a 100th anniversary," he says. "But I'll still contend that even through all the changes, Sun has maintained its traditional values."

Bob Dunlop agrees. He sees the recent changes as one of personality more than character. Personality is an aura reflecting an individual leader. Character is fundamental.

"And," he believes, "the fundamentals on which this company was built have not changed."

In 1951, Sun employees in and around Forsan, Texas, gathered with their families for a company picnic. Forsan was one of Sun's oldest West Texas fields.

The 1985 Marcus Hook men's bowling team carries on the camaraderie and team spirit that has always been an important part of the Sun experience.

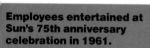

Employees entertained at Sun's 75th anniversary celebration in 1961.

Sun's Glen Dale orchestra musicians played at dances given by the 1608 Club, Philadelphia employee social organization, during the 1950s and '60s.

Robert McClements, Jr.
President 1981-

When he was named chief executive officer of Sun in 1985, a national business magazine referred to Bob McClements as "an oil man to the core."

Considering that all of his training and the early years of his professional life were spent in heavy construction, this assessment by the business press is a tribute to McClements' ability to immerse himself in the job at hand.

For the last two decades Bob McClements has indeed been the epitome of an oil man. And this follows one of his own oft-repeated tenets of corporate life:

He believes that "the most promotable person is not necessarily the one with lofty career ambitions, but the one who is excelling in the job of the moment."

Bob McClements with President Ronald Reagan at White House reception.

McClements' own jobs of the moment for the last two decades have centered on energy resource development.

A civil engineering graduate of Drexel University, Bob McClements was directing construction of Sun's Canadian oil sands mining and processing facility at Fort McMurray, Alberta, in 1965 when he was approached by Sun to become the first general manager of that prototype plant.

In taking that Sun job, he became the first man to both build and manage a commercial synthetic fuel manufacturing plant.

He was transferred to Philadelphia six years later and moved into the mainstream of Sun executive management, first as director of materials management, then as director of engineering.

In 1975, McClements went to Dallas and began setting up the management team that was to put Sun into the coal business for the first time.

As president of Sunoco Energy Development Co., Bob McClements was responsible for opening in

. . . relaxing at home with some of the family pets.

... touring the Tulsa, Okla., refinery with plant manager Tom McCollough.

Wyoming the company's first coal mine. This in turn, led to the acquisition of a group of Eastern coal mines about the time McClements was recalled to Sun's headquarters in Radnor, Pa., made an executive vice president of the corporation, and later a member of the board.

In 1981, Bob McClements was named president and chief operating officer of Sun Company and moved in beside Ted Burtis to help reshape the corporation into a vigorous developer and producer of energy resources.

In 1985 Burtis moved McClements into the additional role of chief executive officer.

An ardent admirer of J. Howard Pew, McClem-ents had the opportunity of meeting with him often back in Canada during the 1960s, while managing the oil sands plant.

"Any company has to have a leader with certain entrepreneurial instincts who provides the sense of purpose for the corporation," says McClements. "In Sun's case that was clearly J. Howard Pew."

McClements has been described as "most of all,

... enjoying an opportunity to talk of the oil business.

a builder." He acknowledges that even in his personal life his favorite form of relaxation is a hands-on building project to sweat over.

"You can do an awful lot of good thinking when you are hammering nails," he says. "It's the type of thing I enjoy getting involved in. I'm saving golf for my old age."

When asked about his vision of Sun in the years ahead, he notes that the company "has shown its mettle over the last 100 years and I have no doubt we'll be around for another 100.

"Maybe our shape will be slightly different," he adds, "but we'll still have that entrepreneurial flair; we'll be dominantly driven by technology and we'll be managed and operated by a group of employees who also have that entrepreneurial outlook."

any deal Sun ventured into would have to be a good business proposition first. But it also had to be business done in an ethical way.

Bob Donahue recalls that when he was in commercial development at Sun, "We posed, not too seriously, the idea of buying a liquor manufacturing company. I just threw it up as a trial balloon, but I thought the Pews would object to the fact that it was liquor. That wasn't it at all. They objected because, at that time, somewhere down the line in the distribution system, organized crime was rumored to be involved."

The fact that manufacturing was very profitable and had nothing to do with distribution made no difference. Mr. Pew would have none of it.

Formed in a gentler time, Sun's business style remains a solid strength in the modern business milieu. Its values are as lasting as its success, and perhaps partly responsible for it.

Sun people not only get energy out (of the ground), they also put energy back (in the community).

Louise Smith (right), Tulsa

Dottie Kidd (center), Dallas

Tom Glessner, Retiree

... touring the Tulsa, Okla., refinery with plant manager Tom McCollough.

Wyoming the company's first coal mine. This in turn, led to the acquisition of a group of Eastern coal mines about the time McClements was recalled to Sun's headquarters in Radnor, Pa., made an executive vice president of the corporation, and later a member of the board.

In 1981, Bob McClements was named president and chief operating officer of Sun Company and moved in beside Ted Burtis to help reshape the corporation into a vigorous developer and producer of energy resources.

In 1985 Burtis moved McClements into the additional role of chief executive officer.

An ardent admirer of J. Howard Pew, McClements had the opportunity of meeting with him often back in Canada during the 1960s, while managing the oil sands plant.

"Any company has to have a leader with certain entrepreneurial instincts who provides the sense of purpose for the corporation," says McClements. "In Sun's case that was clearly J. Howard Pew."

McClements has been described as "most of all,

... enjoying an opportunity to talk of the oil business.

a builder." He acknowledges that even in his personal life his favorite form of relaxation is a hands-on building project to sweat over.

"You can do an awful lot of good thinking when you are hammering nails," he says. "It's the type of thing I enjoy getting involved in. I'm saving golf for my old age."

When asked about his vision of Sun in the years ahead, he notes that the company "has shown its mettle over the last 100 years and I have no doubt we'll be around for another 100.

"Maybe our shape will be slightly different," he adds, "but we'll still have that entrepreneurial flair; we'll be dominantly driven by technology and we'll be managed and operated by a group of employees who also have that entrepreneurial outlook."

"**I** guess I've heard the phrase, 'Let's do what's right,' gosh, I don't know how many times in my career with Sun," says M.D. (Zeke) Noble, retired president of Sun Exploration Company. "There was never any question in my mind what they meant when they said 'Let's do what's right.'"

As Sun Trading's Joe Colella puts it: "Sun stands by its word."

"The credibility, integrity and willingness to share the pain and the glory make us a unique group of people," notes W. J. (Wib) Magers, retired senior vice president.

No mystery about how all that got started. It started because the Pew family didn't leave their principles in church on Sunday morning. They also put them to work on Monday. The culture of Sun Company was molded as the Pews were: to be honest, enterprising, smart and concerned.

In a rough and grimy industry, Sun has cornered for itself a special reputation. Sun people have a reputation for being honest, reliable and cooperative. And Sun is known as a company in which its people can make a deal on a handshake.

"A handshake was every bit as binding as a written agreement," confirms J. Colbert (Pinky) Peurifoy, who retired as manager of the company's western coal division in 1982 after 34 years with Sun. Most agreements with landowners, he recalls, were made over the telephone and followed by a written agreement.

"We never backed out of a lease agreement even if we found out later the agreement was not in the best interests of Sun."

Bob Russ, Toledo refinery

Bill Gill, Retiree

Gary Chadduck, Cordero

Sun volunteers give lessons in good citizenship by working with non-profit community organizations all over the country.

In the 1930s during the heady days of drilling the enormously productive East Texas oil field there was plenty of opportunity to make money quick and dirty, and plenty of people did. The oil flowed in gushers. Drillers flocked in from all over the country.

Many of the newcomers were lucky enough to become millionaires. Sometimes they got there by a crooked path: by running hot oil. That was oil above the production limit set for each company by the Texas Railroad Commission.

"We could have overproduced and run hot oil," says Cecil Colville. But at Sun, the word went out from Jack Pew clear and simple: "You cheat, you're fired."

Samuel K. White, Sun's first general counsel, who kept watch over the company's legal affairs for several years, saw to it that Sun was just as clean in the antitrust area.

"We had very strict rules about talking with competitors about price increases," he says. "Sun had a reputation in the industry for not dealing in such things. Other companies knew that."

This is one of the reasons Bob Hauptfuhrer joined the company 28 years ago. Now president of Sun Exploration and Production Company, he says, "Sun had an outstanding reputation for the ethical way it carried out its business affairs and its relationships with its employees, customers and communities."

This doesn't mean Sun turned its back when it caught the scent of a good opportunity. Of course,

89

any deal Sun ventured into would have to be a good business proposition first. But it also had to be business done in an ethical way.

Bob Donahue recalls that when he was in commercial development at Sun, "We posed, not too seriously, the idea of buying a liquor manufacturing company. I just threw it up as a trial balloon, but I thought the Pews would object to the fact that it was liquor. That wasn't it at all. They objected because, at that time, somewhere down the line in the distribution system, organized crime was rumored to be involved."

The fact that manufacturing was very profitable and had nothing to do with distribution made no difference. Mr. Pew would have none of it.

Formed in a gentler time, Sun's business style remains a solid strength in the modern business milieu. Its values are as lasting as its success, and perhaps partly responsible for it.

Louise Smith (right), Tulsa

Dottie Kidd (center), Dallas

Tom Glessner, Retiree

The latest heroes: (standing) Daniel Majdecki, Toledo refinery; Thomas O'Malley, Aviation Department; Benjamin Almaguer, Toledo refinery; (seated) Albert Floryancic, Bridgeport, Conn., terminal; Joan Grudier, Toledo refinery.

The first: Val Zdun (left) receiving award from J. Howard Pew. Center is Norman Walls, captain of the *M.S. Sun.*

On May 25, 1945, Val Zdun of Sun's Marine Department became the first recipient of the J. Howard Pew Award, established to recognize "an act of heroism beyond the call of duty" on the part of Sun employees.

On Nov. 5, 1985, five more names were added to the list of authentic Sun heroes.

These last presentations bring to just 19 the number of people who have received the Pew award since its inception in 1944.

In addition to those pictured, they are:

- John McKenna, 1957, Marine Department.
- Gerald Flowers, 1957, Production Department.
- Donald Schultz, 1964, Toledo Refinery.
- Junior Davenport, 1964, Toledo Refinery.
- Marvin Cercy (posthumous), 1969, Tulsa Refinery.
- Fred Powell, 1969, Corpus Christi Refinery.
- Allen Enos, 1971, Providence District.
- Marc Cote, 1973, Montreal District.
- Walter Brooks, 1973, Portland District.
- Armand Aubin, 1976, Providence Terminal.
- Juan Rivera, 1976, Yabucoa, Puerto Rico.
- M. Joan Vandeventer, 1978, SPPC.
- Steve Schmitter, 1982, Sun Transport, Inc.

Ted Burtis

"**S**un Company has been, from the very beginning, intensely interested in America."

The man who said that is William Scranton, former Sun board member who was the company's first outside director, as well as Governor of Pennsylvania and Ambassador to the United Nations. A lot of other people would endorse it.

Clyde Wheeler certainly would. As vice president for government relations, Wheeler was in charge of tending Sun's relationships with the federal government. His charge from headquarters was always clear — and consistent with his own values. "We put the country first and the company second," he says.

Sun's way of being patriotic has never been simply to stay out of trouble. "We had a reputation for insisting on having our say," says Wheeler, now retired.

J. Howard Pew believed in individual freedom with a passion and resisted government encroachment on that freedom. Free enterprise wasn't just a matter of self-interest for him; it was a matter of principle.

In a 1948 speech, he said: "When a people come to look upon their government as the source of all their rights, there will surely come a time when they will look upon that same government as the source of all their wrongs."

He continued: "Freedom is indivisible. Once industrial freedom is lost, political freedom, religious freedom, freedom of the press and of speech will all fall."

In the 1970s, when corporations were given the okay to support political candidates, Sun was among the first companies to do so. SunPAC remains an effective vehicle for pooling contributions by Sun employees and shareholders to support the election of candidates for Congress who support the free enterprise system.

In communities where Sun operates, the company supports health, education, arts and cultural organizations with millions in contributions each year.

Sun people add value to the company's dollar contributions by putting their personal time and effort into community and political activities. Maybe it's flying a sick child to needed treatment on the company plane. Maybe it's a scout troop. Maybe it's heading a United Way campaign. One concerted community effort at Sun is the Responsible Citizenship Program, where Sun people give their energy back to the community in a variety of social and political works.

Donald P. Walsh, senior vice president and general counsel, points out that "it's not just that Sun encourages people to be involved . . . this company *expects* a degree of community participation on the part of its employees."

In 1953, Sun vice president W. T. (Tex) Askew (seated left) spearheaded Sun's United Way efforts. In 1984 Chairman Ted Burtis led the Philadelphia-area campaign, which kicked off with a Sun-sponsored street fair.

A corporation today is more than an economic institution. It touches people's lives as employees, consumers, stockholders. It affects the life of the community where it operates. It interacts with units of government to forge policies that encourage the nation's economic growth.

All of which gives a corporation power that few other institutions have. At Sun, tradition directs that that power be used in a benign and befitting way. Not just to keep faith with the past, but also to give a solid foundation to the best possibilities for the future.

That, we can guess, might have been what J. Howard Pew had in mind when he so often repeated the lines from *"The Bridge Builder:"*

"There followeth after me today
A youth whose feet will pass this way . . .
He, too, must cross in the twilight dim.
Good friend, I am building this bridge for him."

Sun has been part of the American scene for nearly half of this nation's history. With pride and gratitude, installations all over Sun display America's colors.

This team of employees carried the momentum of enthusiasm, hallmark of Sun's progress for all of its first 100 years, to the Battle of the Corporate Stars athletic competition.

One was created in the hearts of the French people. The other in the minds of two men. The Statue of Liberty and the Sun Company. Both in 1886.

A century later the Statue continues as a lasting symbol of human freedom. And Sun Company continues as a proud example of what that freedom can produce.